Framing and Being Framed

The Nova Scotia Series—
Source Materials of the Contemporary Arts
Editor: Kasper Koenig

Hans Haacke
Framing and Being Framed
7 Works 1970-75

With Essays by

Jack Burnham
Steps in the Formulation of Real-Time Political Art

Howard S. Becker and John Walton
Social Science and the Work of Hans Haacke

The Press of the Nova Scotia College of Art and Design, Halifax
New York University Press, New York

ISBN: 0-919616-07-0 (Cloth)
       0-919616-08-9 (Paper)
SBN: 0-8147-3370-0 (Cloth, U.S. Edition)
       0-8147-3371-9 (Paper, U.S. Edition)
Library of Congress Catalog Card Number: 75-27103

Manufactured in U.S.A.

Published by the Press of the Nova Scotia College of Art and Design
5163 Duke Street, Halifax, N.S., Canada

Co-published by New York University Press
21 West 4th Street, New York, N.Y. 10012, U.S.A.

Contents

Editor's Note

Framing and Being Framed differs from the editorial policy of the Nova Scotia Series — the publication of source materials of the contemporary arts — in that it also includes contributions other than by the artist-author. In the previous titles of the series the ideas and works of the author were the sole subjects of the books.

The particular emphasis in this volume is on the interface of art, the producers of works of art, their public and their economic and ideological support structure which many of Haacke's works have dealt with over the last five years (the real-estate pieces which were rejected for exhibition by the Guggenheim Museum in 1971, are not included, because they themselves do not refer to the art-system). His works often constitute voluminous and detailed reading material which is not easily taken in, digested, and retained while standing up and reading off a gallery wall. It is in a gallery or a museum, though, where they attain a socio-economic and political impregnation which then becomes an essential part of these works. Once they have been exposed to this fertilization, as all works reproduced here have, they retain the specific contextual quality, even if they are no longer seen in the environment for which they were originally made. The exclusive publication in bookform would deprive Haacke's pieces of that context in which their full

signification and potential as irritant is achieved.

We agreed that the artist should maintain his aloofness and abstain from commenting his own works.

In order to elucidate their social setting in the contemporary art system, and their use of methods commonly associated with social science, rather than art, we requested contributions from a social scientist as well as an art writer.

Jack Burnham, a long-time friend of Hans Haacke, accepted our invitation to provide information on his background and development and to evaluate his activities. While casting about for a contribution by a social scientist, it was Jack Burnham who suggested Howard S. Becker who, in turn, secured the cooperation of John Walton, also from Northwestern University.

To maintain their actual appearance Haacke's seven pieces are reproduced scaled down in facsimile. All additional material by the artist, other than the pieces, is set in Univers typeface. The articles are set in Times Roman.

Kasper Koenig
Halifax, August, 1975

7

MOMA-Poll

From June 20 through September 20, 1970, the Museum of Modern Art in New York held an exhibition entitled *Information.* Organized by Curator Kynaston McShine, it was to give, in his words, an "international report of the activity of younger artists" comprising the work of approximately 90 artists. The exhibition was installed in the Museum's ground floor galleries.

Invited to participate in the *Information* show, I entered a proposal according to which visitors were requested to answer an either-or question referring to a current socio-political issue. They would cast a ballot into one of two transparent ballot boxes marked respectively "yes" and "no". The proposal was accepted, but I did not hand in the question until the evening before the opening of the exhibition.

The ballot boxes, each equipped with a photoelectrically triggered counting device registering all pieces of paper dropped into the box, were installed in the first room of the show. The question was posted above them.

Each visitor was given a ballot at the entrance. The color of the ballots differed according to his/her status as a full-paying visitor, a member of the Museum, a holder of a courtesy pass, or a visitor who came on Monday, the one day of the week when admission to the Museum was free. Every evening a member of the Museum's staff was to enter the tally of the various classes of visitors and the number of ballots in the two ballot boxes on a chart posted next to them.

In effect, ballots were not handed out regularly or according to the color code as directed. Consequently some visitors cast improvised ballots of torn paper.

On September 20, at the close of the 12 week exhibition, the automatic counting devices of the ballot boxes had registered:

Yes: 25,566 (68.7%)

No: 11,563 (31.3%)

Participation was 37,129, that is 12.4% of all the 299,057 visitors of the Museum of Modern Art during that period (including those who did not see the *Information* show).

More than 153,433 visitors (figures for 5 days are missing) paid an admission fee of $1.50 or $1.75 (admission was raised August 7), totalling more than $136,995.25.

Admission by courtesy passes or membership cards amounted to 67,312; free entries on Mondays and certain evenings 67,057.

At the time of the *Information* show, David Rockefeller was the Chairman of the Board of Trustees of the Museum of Modern Art. His brother, Nelson Rockefeller, then the incumbent Governor of New York State, was also a member of the Board, and so was their sister-in-law Mrs. John D. Rockefeller 3rd. The Museum's treasurer was Willard C. Butcher, then the Executive Vice President of the Chase Manhattan Bank, of which David Rockefeller was and is Chairman. The Director of the Museum was John Hightower. He had been the Executive Director of the New York State Council of the Arts, a position to which he had been appointed by Governor Nelson Rockefeller. Mr. Hightower had also accompanied Nelson Rockefeller on a stormy political tour of South America undertaken at the request of President Nixon.

Two months before the opening of the exhibition, U.S. Forces under the direction of President Nixon had bombed and invaded Cambodia. Large demonstrations were held all over the U.S. in protest against this policy. During one of these demonstrations, on the campus of Kent State University, 4 students were shot to death by National Guardsmen.

Question:

Would the fact that Governor Rockefeller
has not denounced President Nixon's
Indochina policy be a reason for you not
to vote for him in November ?

Answer:

If 'yes'
please cast your ballot into the left box
if 'no'
into the right box.

John Weber Gallery Visitors' Profile 1

John Weber Gallery Visitors' Profile 1

1972. 21 blueprints, 24″ × 30″ (61 × 76 cm).

First exhibited in one-man show at John Weber Gallery, New York, May 1972. Mounted on wall with masking tape.

Edition of 3. All owned by H.H.

These questions and your answers are part of

420 WEST BROADWAY VISITORS' PROFILE

a work in progress by Hans Haacke at the John Weber Gallery, October 7 through 24, 1972

Please fill out this questionnaire and drop it into the box provided for this. Dont sign!

---

1) Do you have a professional interest in art (e.g. artist, dealer, critic, etc.)?   Yes ___ No ___

2) Where do you live?   City _____   County _____   State _____

3) It has been suggested that artists and museum staff members be represented on the Board of Trustees oft art museums. Do you think this is a good idea?   Yes ___ No ___ Dont know ___

4) How old are you?   ___ years

5) If elections were held today, for which presidential candidate would you vote?
                                                Mc Govern ___   Nixon ___   None ___   Dont know ___

6) In your opinion, are the interests of profit-oriented business usually compatible with the common good?
                                                                        Yes ___ No ___ Dont know ___

7) What is your annual income(before taxes)? $ _____

8) Do you think present US taxation favors large incomes or low incomes, or is distributing the burden correctly?
                                        Favors large incomes ___   Favors low incomes ___   correct ___

9) What is your occupation?   _____

10) Would you bus your child to integrate schools?   Yes ___ No ___ Dont know ___

11) Do you have children?   Yes ___ No ___

12) What is the country of origin of your ancestors (e.g. Africa, England, Italy, Poland etc.)? _____

13) Esthetic questions aside, which of these New York museums would in your opinion exhibit works critical of the present US Government?

    Brooklyn Museum ___   Finch College Museum ___   Guggenheim Museum ___   Jewish Museum ___   Metropolitan Museum ___   Museum of Modern Art ___   New York Cultural Center ___   Whitney Museum ___   All museums ___   None of these museums ___   Dont know ___

14) Are you enrolled in or have you graduated from college?   Yes ___ No ___

15) Assuming the prescriptions of the M.I.T. (club of Rome) study for the survival of mankind are correct, do you think the capitalist system of the US is better suited for achieving the state of almost zero economic growth required than other socio-economic systems?
                                                                        Yes ___ No ___ Dont know ___

16) Do you think civil liberties in the US are being eroded, have been increasingly respected, or have not gained or lost during the past few years?
                                        Eroded ___   Increasingly respected ___   Not gained or lost ___

17) What is your religion?   Catholic ___   Protestant ___   Jewish ___   Other ___   None ___

18) Sex?   Male ___   Female ___

19) Do you think the bombing of North Vietnam favors, hurts, or has no effect on the chances for peace in Indochina?
                                        Favors ___   Hurts ___   No effect ___   Dont know ___

20) Do you consider yourself politically a conservative, liberal or radical?
                                        Conservative ___   Liberal ___   Radical ___   Dont know ___

Thank you for your cooperation. Your answers will be tabulated with the answers of all other visitors. The results will be posted during the exhibition.

15

During an exhibition of works by Carl Andre, Hans Haacke, Nancy Holt, Laurie James, Brenda Miller and Mary Obering, October 7 through 24, 1972, the visitors of the John Weber Gallery were requested by Hans Haacke to complete a questionnaire with 20 questions. 10 of these questions inquired about their demographic background and 10 questions related to the visitors' opinions on socio-political issues. They were either multiple choice questions or had to be answered by writing in a figure or a word. The questionnaires were provided in 2 file trays sitting on either end of a long table in the gallery, together with pencils. The completed forms were dropped into a wooden box with a slit in the top. Throughout the exhibition intermediate results of the survey were posted on the nearby wall.

During the time of the polling, the other galleries sharing the same address with the John Weber Gallery at 420 West Broadway in New York's Soho district, had the following exhibitions: "New Works by Artists" (Judd, Morris, Nauman, Rauschenberg, Serra, Stella) at the Castelli Gallery, Jannis Kounellis at the Sonnabend Gallery and Sylvia Stone at the Emmerich Gallery. The public of each of these galleries usually also visits the other exhibitions in the building.

In the tabulation, all blanks and answers not conforming to the multiple choice of answers offered in the questionnaire, were counted as "no answer". Except for 2 questions that allowed for more than one answer, all multiple answers to a single question were equally counted as "no answer". The figures were translated into percent with decimals rounded to the nearest full number. Approximately 1.5% of the 858 questionnaires contained one or more answers that were not to be taken seriously. However, these were not eliminated in the computation.

858 questionnaires were completed during the 13 days of the exhibition. Since the total number of visitors is unknown, the ratio of participation cannot be ascertained. It is open to speculation whether nonparticipating visitors differed essentially in their demographic backgrounds and opinions. The results of the survey are only a representation of the 858 who have completed the questionnaire. For these, however, it is a full representation, a profile not based on samplings. It cannot claim to give a picture of all visitors of the John Weber Gallery, of the public of other galleries, or the art public at large.

The pie chart shows the proportional breakdown of the total visitors polled into 4 constituent subgroups. It adds up to 100%.

The bar graphs visualize the proportional distribution of answers given by the total visitors polled (black bar) and compare it with the relations within each of the 4 subgroups, the visitors with no professional interest in art (cross hatched bar), visitors declaring themselves artists (grid bar) and students with a professional interest in art (white bar). Thus each answer-block of 5 bars allows the reader to recognize how the subgroups' characteristics resemble or differ from each other and how each one compares with the response of the total visitors polled. Focussing on any one of the groups by following the bar representing it in each of the answer-blocks, one can see how all answers are distributed proportionally within that group. 100% always represents the sum of all bars of the same color (all answers given by one group).

Hans Haacke

Do you have a professional interest in art (e.g. artist, dealer, critic, etc.)?

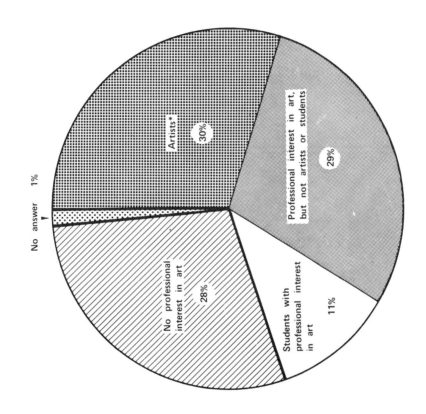

No answer 1%

Artists* 30%

Professional interest in art, but not artists or students 29%

No professional interest in art 28%

Students with professional interest in art 11%

*Only those declaring themselves "artists", "painters", "sculptors" were counted as "artists".

Where do you live ?

Graphs compare relative residential distribution, in percent, within each category of visitors polled.

3% of total visitors polled gave no answer to this question

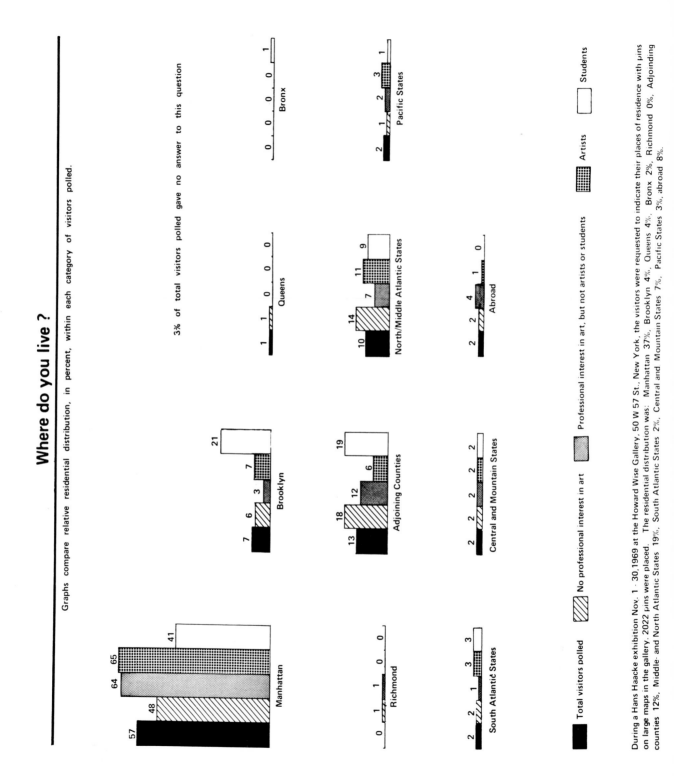

During a Hans Haacke exhibition Nov. 1 - 30, 1969 at the Howard Wise Gallery, 50 W 57 St., New York, the visitors were requested to indicate their places of residence with pins on large maps in the gallery. 2022 pins were placed. The residential distribution was: Manhattan 37%, Brooklyn 4%, Queens 4%, Bronx 2%, Richmond 0%, Adjoinding counties 12%, South Atlantic States 19%, Central and Mountain States 2%, Pacific States 7%, Pacific States 3%, abroad 8%.

It has been suggested that artists and museum staff members be represented on the Board of Trustees of art museums. Do you think this is a good idea ?

Graphs compare relative distribution of opinions, in percent, within each category of visitors polled

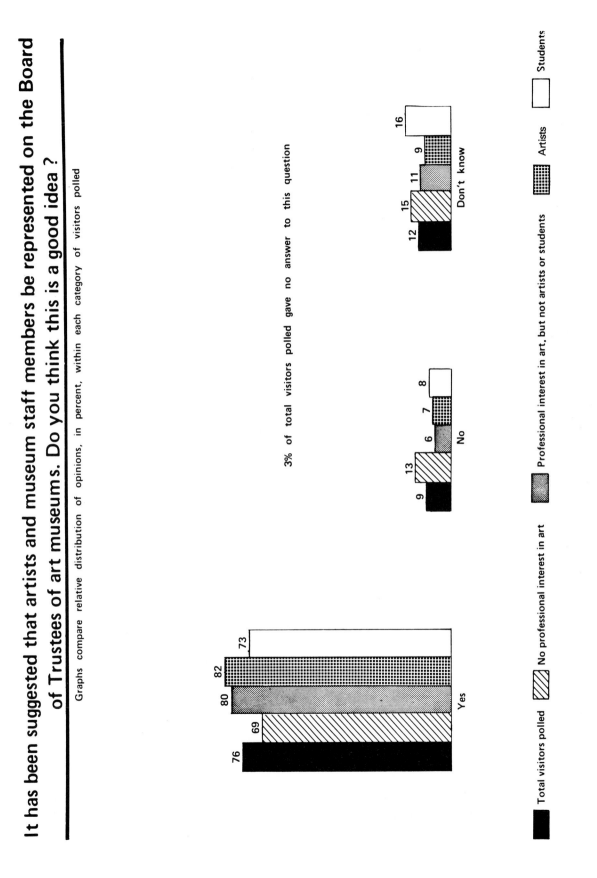

3% of total visitors polled gave no answer to this question

Total visitors polled   **No professional interest in art**   **Professional interest in art, but not artists or students**   **Artists**   **Students**

How old are you ?

Graphs compare relative distribution of age, in percent, within each category of visitors polled

3% of total visitors polled gave no answer to this question

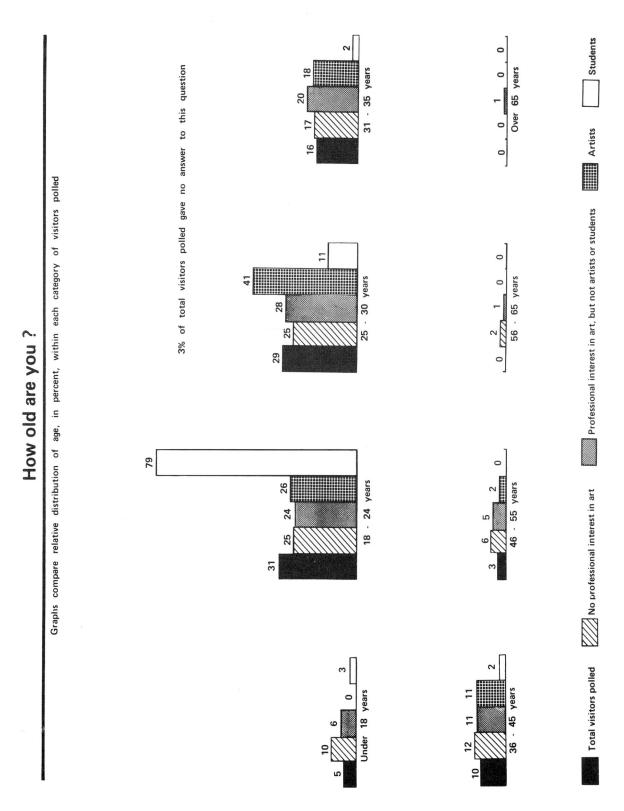

If elections were held today, for which presidential candidate would you vote ?

Graphs compare relative distribution of vote, in percent, within each category of visitors polled

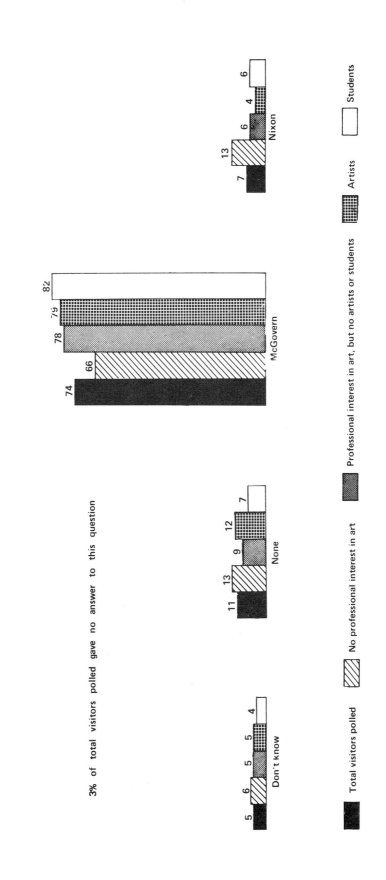

3% of total visitors polled gave no answer to this question

Nixon
6 4 6 13 7

McGovern
82 79 78 66 74

None
7 12 9 13 11

Don't know
4 5 5 6 5

■ Total visitors polled

▨ No professional interest in art

▧ Professional interest in art, but no artists or students

▦ Artists

□ Students

21

In your opinion, are the interests of profit - oriented business usually compatible with the common good ?

Graphs compare relative distribution of opinions, in percent, within each category of visitors polled

6% of total visitors polled gave no answer to this question

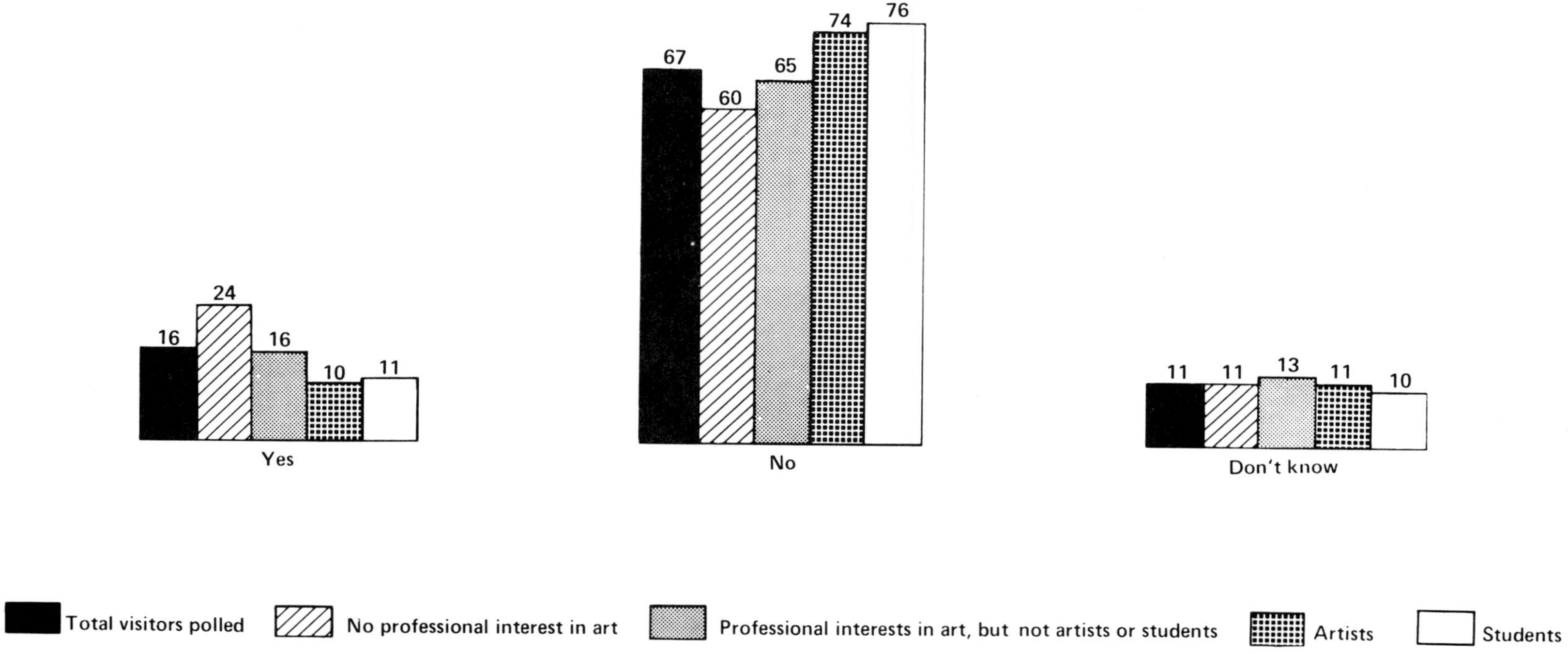

Yes

16   24   16   10   11

No

67   60   65   74   76

Don't know

11   11   13   11   10

Total visitors polled

No professional interest in art

Professional interests in art, but not artists or students

Artists

Students

What is your annual income (before taxes) ?

Graphs compare relative distribution of income, in percent, within each category of visitors polled

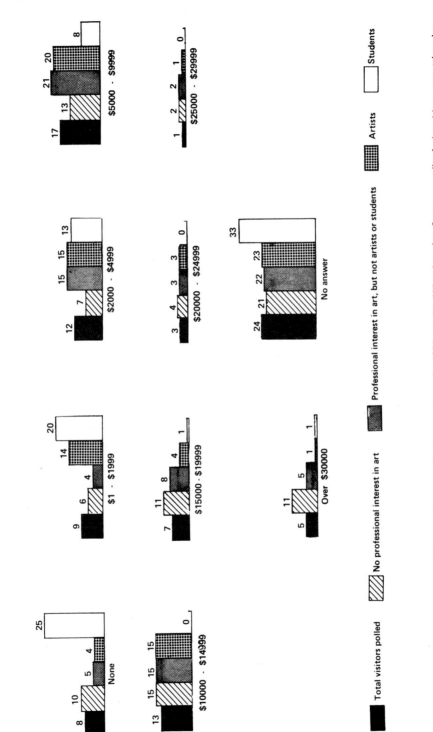

During the exhibition "Directions 3: Eight Artists", June 19 through August 8, 1971, at the Milwaukee Art Center, a poll of the visitors was taken by Hans Haacke. They were asked to complete a questionnaire of 20 questions. 4547 visitors(12%) responded. Their distribution of income was: Under $2000 30%, $2000 - $4999 30%, $5000 - $9999 6%, $10000 - $25000 12%, over $25000 14%. 9% of the visitors polled gave no answer to this question

Do you think US taxation favors large incomes or low incomes, or is distributing the burden correctly?

Graphs compare relative distribution of opinions, in percent, within each category of visitors polled

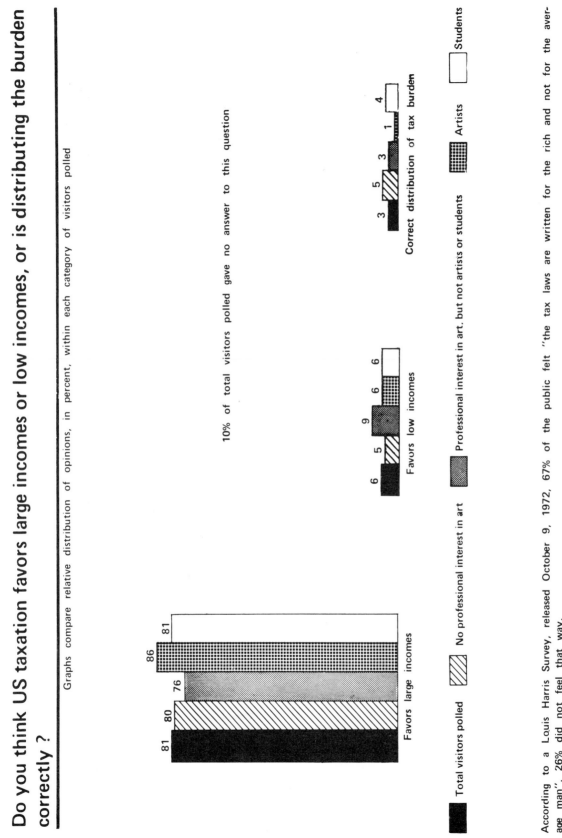

10% of total visitors polled gave no answer to this question

Favors large incomes — 81, 80, 76, 86, 81

Favors low incomes — 6, 5, 9, 6, 6

Correct distribution of tax burden — 3, 5, 3, 1, 4

Total visitors polled

No professional interest in art

Professional interest in art, but not artists or students

Artists

Students

According to a Louis Harris Survey, released October 9, 1972, 67% of the public felt "the tax laws are written for the rich and not for the average man". 26% did not feel that way.

24

What is your occupation ?

Graphs compare relative distribution of professions, in percent, within each category of visitors polled

6% of total visitors polled gave no answer to this question

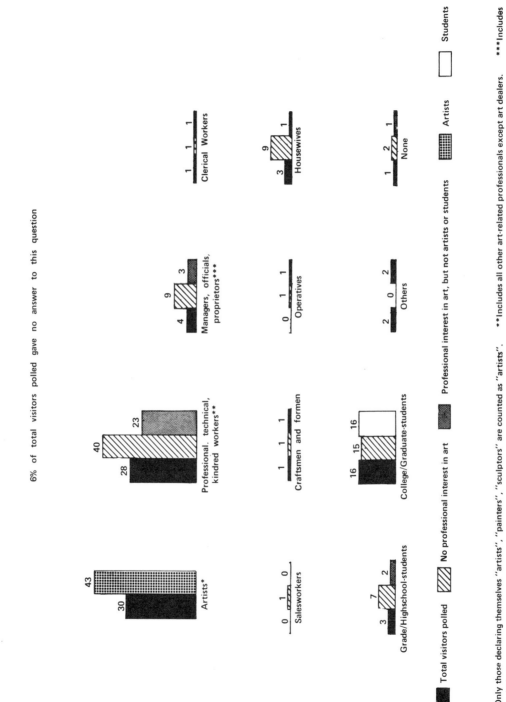

Total visitors polled   No professional interest in art   Professional interest in art, but not artists or students   Artists   Students

*Only those declaring themselves "artists", "painters", "sculptors" are counted as "artists".   **Includes all other art-related professionals except art dealers.   ***Includes art dealers.

Would you bus your child to integrate schools ?

Graphs compare relative distribution of responses, in percent, within each category of visitors polled

7% of total visitors polled gave no answer to this question

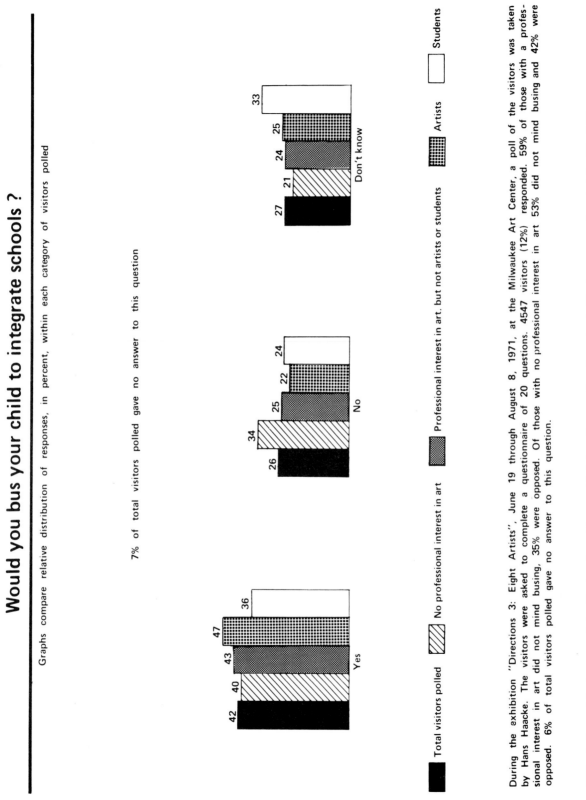

Yes

No

Don't know

□ Total visitors polled

▨ No professional interest in art

▦ Professional interest in art. but not artists or students

▩ Artists

□ Students

During the exhibition "Directions 3: Eight Artists", June 19 through August 8, 1971, at the Milwaukee Art Center, a poll of the visitors was taken by Hans Haacke. The visitors were asked to complete a questionnaire of 20 questions. 4547 visitors (12%) responded. 59% of those with a professional interest in art did not mind busing, 35% were opposed. Of those with no professional interest in art 53% did not mind busing and 42% were opposed. 6% of total visitors polled gave no answer to this question.

81% of the public is opposed to "busing to achieve racial balance", according to a Louis Harris survey, released July 13, 1972.

Do you have children ?

Graphs compare the relative distribution of responses, in percent, within each category of visitors polled

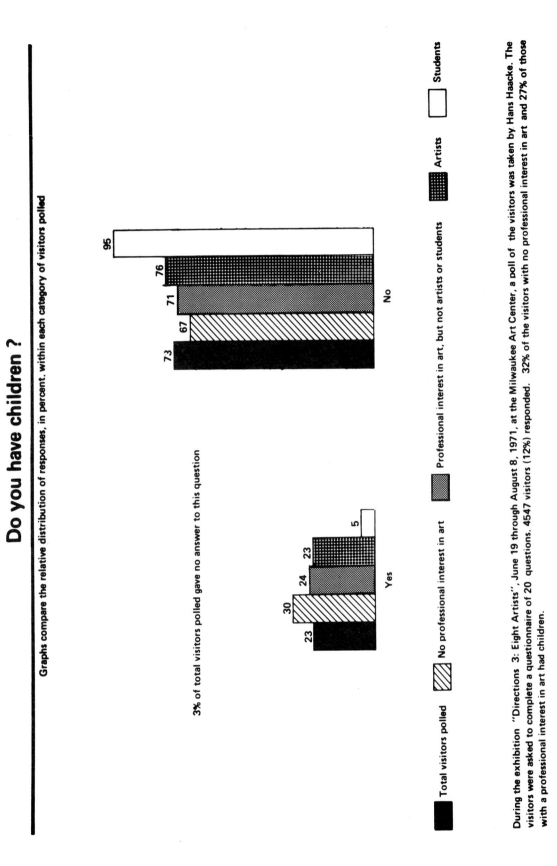

3% of total visitors polled gave no answer to this question

Total visitors polled   **No professional interest in art**   **Professional interest in art, but not artists or students**   **Artists**   **Students**

During the exhibition "Directions 3: Eight Artists", June 19 through August 8, 1971, at the Milwaukee Art Center, a poll of the visitors was taken by Hans Haacke. The visitors were asked to complete a questionnaire of 20 questions. 4547 visitors (12%) responded. 32% of the visitors with no professional interest in art and 27% of those with a professional interest in art had children.

27

What is the country of origin of your ancestors (e.g. Africa, England, Italy, Poland, etc.) ?

Graphs compare relative distribution of ethnic backgrounds, in percent, within each category of visitors polled

When more than one country was given, only the first one mentioned was counted

6% of total visitors polled gave no answer to this question

Total visitors polled

No professional interest in art

Professional interest in art, but not artists or students

Artists

Students

28

Esthetic questions aside, which of these New York museums would in your opinion exhibit works critical of the present US Government?

Graphs compare the relative frequency, in percent, by which any one of the museums was named by each category of visitors polled
More than one museum could be named

3% of total visitors polled gave no answer to this question

Jewish Museum
6 5 8 4 5

Whitney Museum
16 17 17 14 18

Finch College Museum
4 3 9 2 3

New York Cultural Center
4 5 5 3 2

Don't know
30 37 27 25 33

Guggenheim Museum
7 8 8 5 3

Museum of Modern Art
16 18 18 12 20

All museums
5 3 6 5 7

Brooklyn Museum
8 8 11 8 7

Metropolitan Museum
3 2 4 2 1

None of these museums
23 15 21 21 21

Total visitors polled   No professional interest in art   Professional interest in art, but not artists or students   Artists   Students

29

Are your enrolled in or have your graduated from college ?

Graphs compare the relative distribution of college education, in percent, within each category of visitors polled

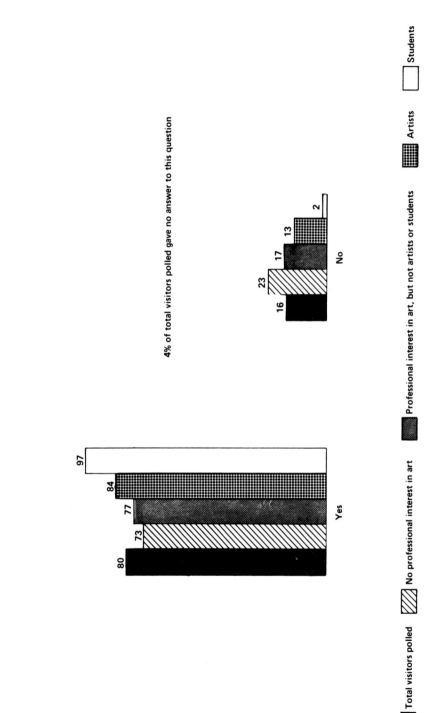

4% of total visitors polled gave no answer to this question

Yes

No

97 84 77 73 80

16 23 17 13 2

Total visitors polled   No professional interest in art   Professional interest in art, but not artists or students   Artists   Students

During the exhibition "Directions 3: Eight Artists", June 19 through August 8, 1971, at the Milwaukee Art Center. a poll of the visitors was taken by Hans Haacke. The visitors were requested to complete a questionnaire of 20 questions.   4547 visitors (12%) responded.   59% of the visitors with no professional interest in art and 39% of those with a professional interest in art were enrolled in or had graduated from college.

30

Assuming the prescriptions of the M.I.T.(Club of Rome) study for the survival of mankind are correct, do you think the capitalist system of the US is better suited for achieving the state of almost zero economic growth required than other socio-economic systems ?

Graphs compare relative distribution of opinions, in percent, within each category of visitors polled

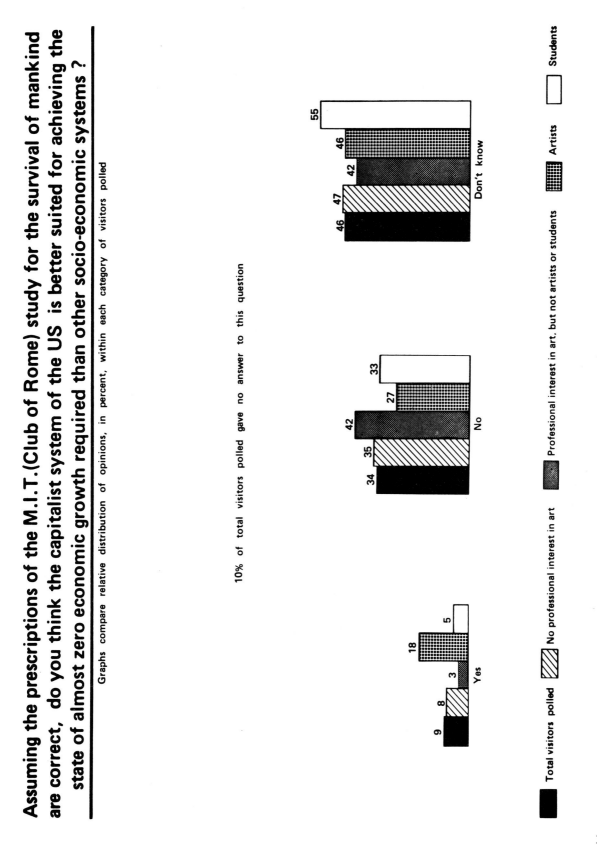

10% of total visitors polled gave no answer to this question

Total visitors polled

No professional interest in art

Professional interest in art, but not artists or students

Artists

Students

Do you think civil liberties in the US are being eroded, have been increasingly respected, or have not gained or lost during the past few years ?

Graphs compare the relative distribution of opinions, in percent, within each category of visitors polled

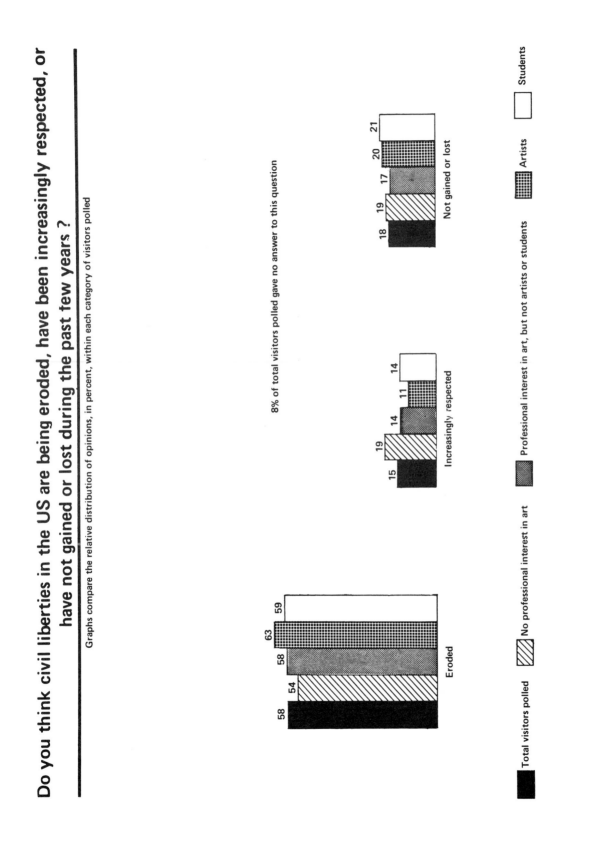

8% of total visitors polled gave no answer to this question

Eroded
58 54 58 63 59

Increasingly respected
15 19 14 11 14

Not gained or lost
18 19 17 20 21

Total visitors polled

No professional interest in art

Professional interest in art, but not artists or students

Artists

Students

What is your religion?

Graphs compare relative distribution of religious affiliation, in percent, within each category of visitors polled

6% of total visitors polled gave no answer to this question

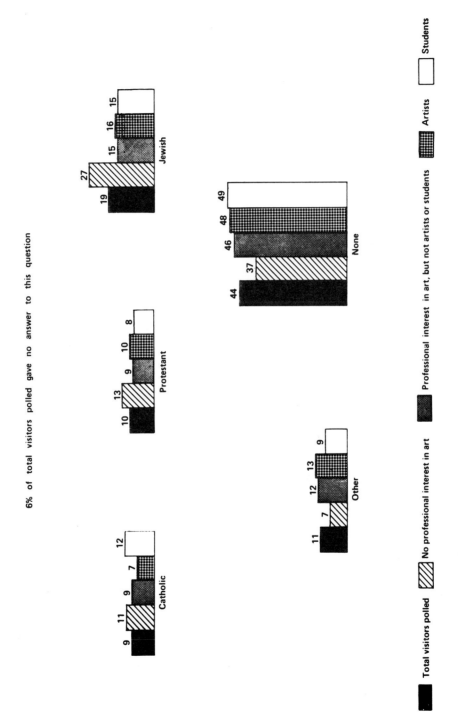

Total visitors polled

No professional interest in art

Professional interest in art, but not artists or students

Artists

Students

During the exhibition "Directions 3 : Eight Artists", June 19 through August 8, 1971, at the Milwaukee Art Center, a poll of the visitors was taken by Hans Haacke. They were asked to complete a questionnaire of 20 questions. 4547 visitors (12%) responded. Their religious affiliation was Catholic 31%, Protestant 11%, Jewish 17%, other 18%, none 4%, no answer 19%.

33

Sex ?

Graphs compare relative distribution of sexes, in percent, within each category of visitors polled

4% of total visitors polled gave no answer to this question

■ Total visitors polled   ▨ No professional interest in art   ▨ Professional interest in art, but not artists or students   ▨ Artists   □ Students

During the exhibition "Directions 3: Eight Artists", June 19 through August 8, 1971, at the Milwaukee Art Center, a poll of the visitors was taken by Hans Haacke. They were asked to complete a questionnaire of 20 questions. 4547 visitors (12%) responded. They were 46% male and 53% female.

According to US Census figures (1971), the population is 49% male and 51% female.

Do you think the bombing of North Vietnam favors, hurts, or has no effect on the chances for peace in Indochina ?

Graphs compare relative distribution of opinions, in percent, within each category of visitors polled

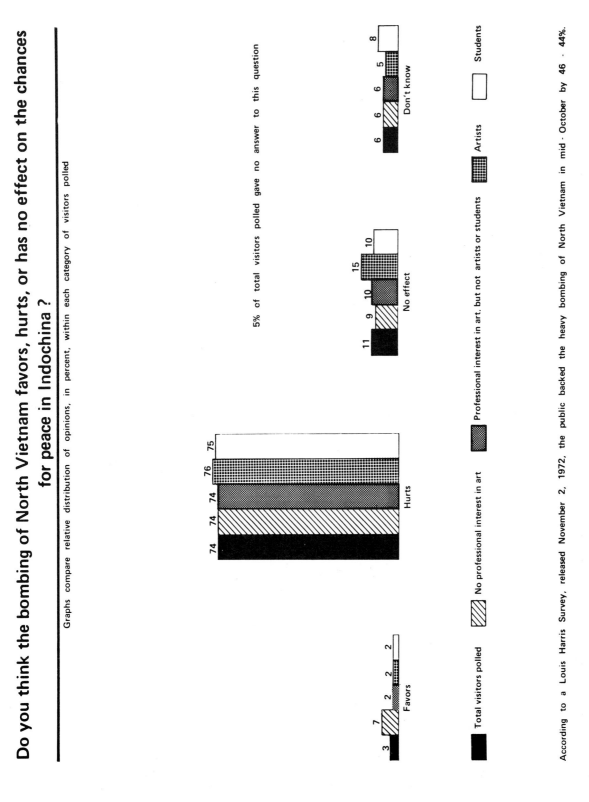

5% of total visitors polled gave no answer to this question

Total visitors polled

No professional interest in art

Professional interest in art. but not artists or students

Artists

Students

According to a Louis Harris Survey, released November 2, 1972, the public backed the heavy bombing of North Vietnam in mid - October by 46 - 44%.

Do you consider yourself politically a conservative, liberal or radical ?

Graphs compare relative distribution of response, in percent, within each category of visitors polled

13% of total visitors polled gave no answer to this question

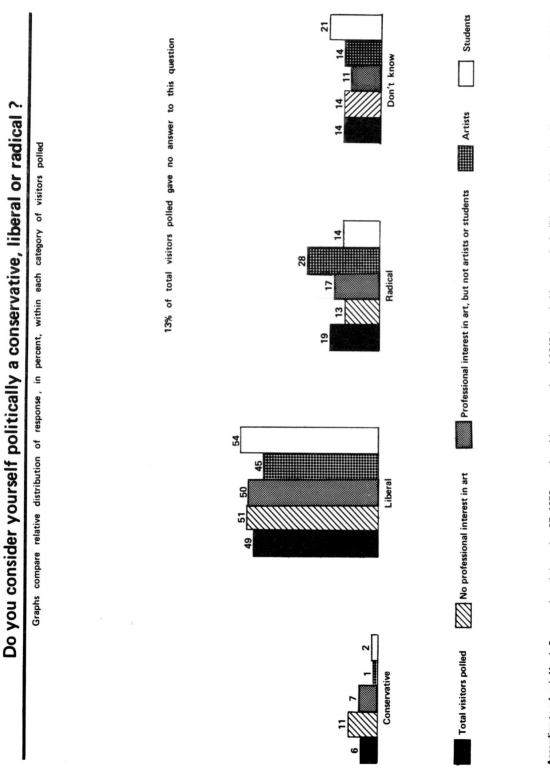

Total visitors polled

No professional interest in art

Professional interest in art, but not artists or students

Artists

Students

According to a Louis Harris Survey, released November 27, 1972, a nationwide cross section of 1648 households were asked: "How would you describe your own political philosophy --- conservative, middle-of-the-road, liberal, or radical?" The response was: Conservative 35%, Middle-of-the-road 34%, Liberal 19%, Radical 3%, Not sure 9% .

John Weber Gallery Visitors' Profile 2

John Weber Gallery Visitors' Profile 2

1972. 29 sheets of drawing-paper, 8½ " × 11" (21.5 × 28 cm).

First exhibited in group show at John Weber Gallery, New York, September 1972.

Owned by H.H.

JOHN WEBER GALLERY VISITORS' PROFILE 2

by Hans Haacke

A work in progress during his exhibition at the J. Weber Galler, 420 W. Broadway, NYC, April 28 — May 17, 1973.

Please answer by punching out bridge between edge and hole next to the answer of your choice.

as artist	Do you have a professional interest in art?	
as art/art history student		
other professional interest		
no professional interest		

What do you think is the approximate proportion of Nixon sympathizers among art museum trustees?

- 100 %
- 75 %
- 50 %
- 25 %
- 0 %
- don't know

Manhattan	Where do you live?
Brooklyn	
Queens	
Bronx	
Richmond	
adjoining counties	
elsewhere North/Middle Atlantic States	
South Atlantic States	
Central and Mountain States	
Pacific States	
abroad	

What do you think is the approximate proportion of Nixon sympathizers among visitors to contemporary art exhibitions?

- 100 %
- 75 %
- 50 %
- 25 %
- 0 %
- don't know

favor	Does your notion of art favor, tolerate, or reject works that make deliberate reference to socio-political things?
tolerate	
reject	
don't know	

What was your personal income in 1972 (before taxes)?

- none
- $1 - 1999
- $2000 - 4999
- $5000 - 9999
- $10000 - 14999
- $15000 - 19999
- $20000 - 24999
- $25000 - 29999
- over $30000

yes, 50 %	Do you think, as a matter of principal, that all group shows should include women artists?
yes, but no specified quota	
sex should be no criterion	
don't know	

Sex?

- male
- female

Continued. ▶

K5S 671B

39

How much money have you spent on buying art(total)?

- none
- $1 – 1999
- $2000 – 4999
- $5000 – 14999
- $15000 – 29999
- over $30000

To whom should the trustees of art museums be accountable(more than one can be named)?

- only to themselves
- patrons of museum
- museum membership
- museum staff
- artists' representatives
- publicly elected officials
- American Association of Museums
- College Art Association
- National Endowment for the Arts
- Associated Councils of the Arts
- foundation representatives
- other(write in) _____
- don't know

Some people say President Nixon is ultimately responsible for the Watergate scheme. Do you agree?

- responsible
- not responsible
- don't know

How would you characterize the socio-economic status of your parents?

- poverty
- lower middle income
- middle income
- upper middle income
- wealthy

What is the religious background of your family?

- Catholic
- Protestant
- Jewish
- other
- mixed
- none

Do you think the preferences of those who financially back the art world influence the kind of work artists produce?

- yes, a lot
- somewhat
- slightly
- not at all
- don't know

Have you ever lived or worked for more than one half year in a poverty area?

- yes
- no

It has been charged that the present U.S. Government is catering to business interests. Do you think this is the case?

- always
- often
- occasionally
- never
- don't know

Do you think the collectors who buy the kind of art you like, share your political/ideological opinions?

- generally yes
- generally no
- don't know

How old are you?

- under 18 years
- 18 - 24 years
- 25 - 30 years
- 31 - 35 years
- 36 - 45 years
- 46 - 55 years
- 56 - 65 years
- over 65 years

Would your standard of living be affected, if no more art of living artists were bought?

- yes
- no
- don't know

Do you daily read the political section of a newspaper?

- yes
- no

Do you think the visitors of the J. Weber Gallery who participated in the poll differed from those who did not?

- very different
- somewhat d.
- essentially same
- don't know

Thank you. Drop the card into the ballot box. Your answers will be tabulated with the answers of all other visitors. Intermediate results will be posted during the exhibition.

During the exhibition of graphs picturing the results of a previous survey of the John Weber Gallery public (taken October 7 - 24, 1972), a second poll was conducted by Hans Haacke April 28 through May 17, 1973 at the John Weber Gallery.

The visitors of the show were requested to answer 21 multiple choice questions, printed on both sides of a key sort card, by punching out the answers of their choice. The questions inquired about the visitors' demographic background and opinions on socio-political and art issues. The questionnaires were provided in 2 file trays sitting on either end of a long table in the center of the exhibition. Punchers were hanging from the ceiling above the table. The punched cards were to be dropped into a wooden box with a slit in the top. Throughout the exhibition intermediate results of the new survey were posted as part of the show.

During the time of the polling, the other galleries sharing the same address with the John Weber Gallery at 420 West Broadway in New York's Soho district, had the following exhibitions: Hanne Darboven at the Castelli Gallery, John Baldessari at the Sonnabend Gallery and Miriam Shapiro at the Emmerich Gallery. Simultaneously to the first part of the Haacke exhibition a show of works by Robert Ryman was held in the front room of the John Weber Gallery. Later this was replaced by Steve Reich's music scores, displayed at the occasion of several con-

certs in the Gallery. The public of each of the galleries in the building usually also visits the exhibitions of the three other galleries.

In the tabulation, all questions without an answer or with mutually exclusive answers were counted as "no answer". Mutilated cards and cards with answers that were obviously not serious were not counted. Figures in percent were rounded to the nearest full number.

1324 questionnaires were tabulated during the 14 days of the exhibition. Since the total number of visitors is unknown, the ratio of participation cannot be ascertained. It is open to speculation whether nonparticipating visitors differed essentially in their demographic backgrounds and opinions. The results are only a representation of the 1324 who responded. For these, however, it is a full representation, a profile not based on samplings.

The significant increase in "no answer" tabulations from question 9 onwards might be explained by the fact that these questions were printed on the back side of the card. The answer "patrons of museum" in question 10 seemed to have been understood in two conflicting ways: as major donors of museums (museum terminology) and as visitors of museums. The write-in answers ("other") for question 10 were all of a very general type (mankind, posterity, art, the artists, the public, etc.) not referring to an organized or otherwise clearly identifiable group able to act as such.

Hans Haacke

Where do you live?

Figures in percent

Manhattan	43
Brooklyn	6
Queens	2
Bronx	1
Richmond	0
adjoining counties	12
elsewhere North/Middle Atlantic States	17
South Atlantic States	2
Central and Maountain States	3
Pacific States	4
abroad	3
no answer	4

Do you have a professional interest in art?

Figures in percent

as artist	47
as art/art history student	14
other professional interest	13
no professional interest	22
no answer	4

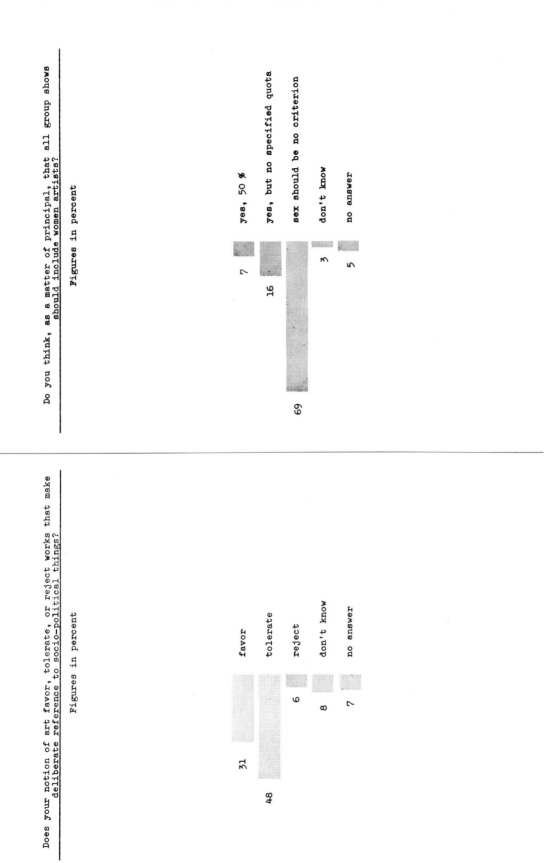

Do you think, as a matter of principal, that all group shows
should include women artists?

Figures in percent

yes, 50 %   7

yes, but no specified quota   16

sex should be no criterion   69

don't know   3

no answer   5

Does your notion of art favor, tolerate, or reject works that make
deliberate reference to socio-political things?

Figures in percent

favor   31

tolerate   48

reject   6

don't know   8

no answer   7

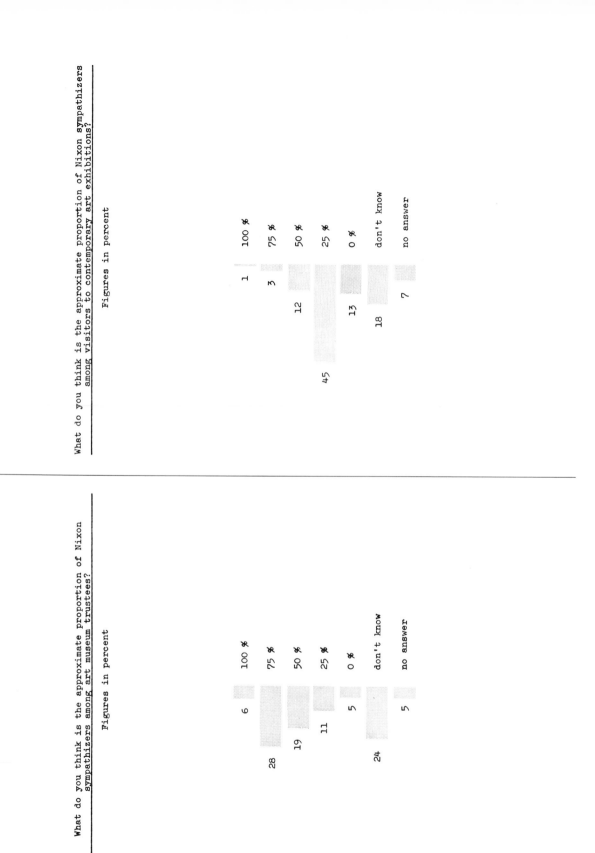

What do you think is the approximate proportion of Nixon sympathizers among art museum trustees?

Figures in percent

6	100 %
28	75 %
19	50 %
11	25 %
5	0 %
24	don't know
5	no answer

What do you think is the approximate proportion of Nixon sympathizers among visitors to contemporary art exhibitions?

Figures in percent

1	100 %
3	75 %
12	50 %
45	25 %
13	0 %
18	don't know
7	no answer

44

Sex?

Figures in percent

male

female

no answer

44

42

14

What was your personal income in 1972(before taxes)?

Figures in percent

$1 – 1999

$2000 – 4999

$5000 – 9999

$10000 – 14999

$15000 – 19999

$20000 – 24999

$25000 – 29999

over $30000

no answer

11

23

16

15

11

5

4

3

6

6

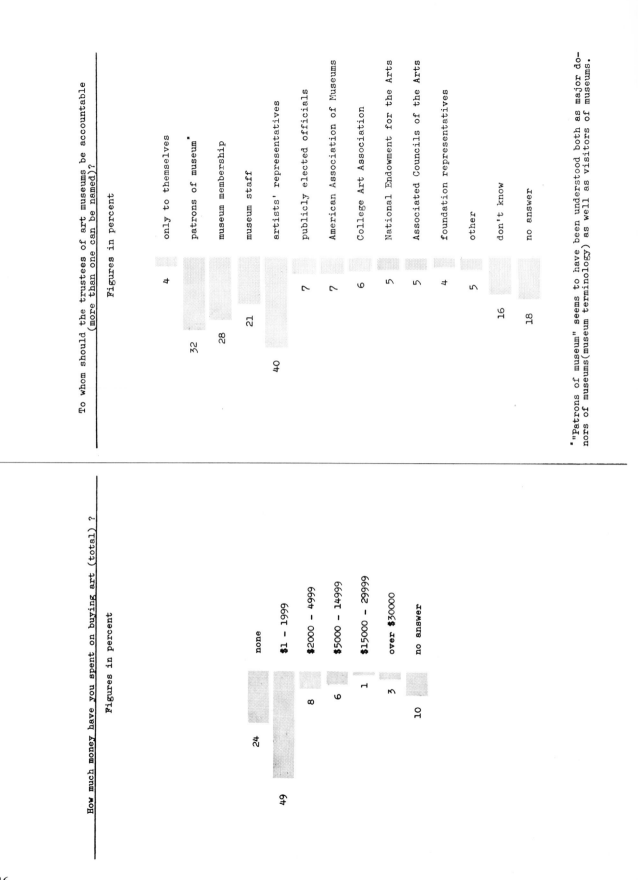

To whom should the trustees of art museums be accountable (more than one can be named)?

Figures in percent

only to themselves	4
patrons of museum "	32
museum membership	28
museum staff	21
artists' representatives	40
publicly elected officials	7
American Association of Museums	7
College Art Association	6
National Endowment for the Arts	5
Associated Councils of the Arts	5
foundation representatives	4
other	5
don't know	16
no answer	18

" "Patrons of museum" seems to have been understood both as major donors of museums(museum terminology) as well as visitors of museums.

How much money have you spent on buying art (total)?

Figures in percent

none	24
$1 - 1999	49
$2000 - 4999	8
$5000 - 14999	6
$15000 - 29999	1
over $30000	3
no answer	10

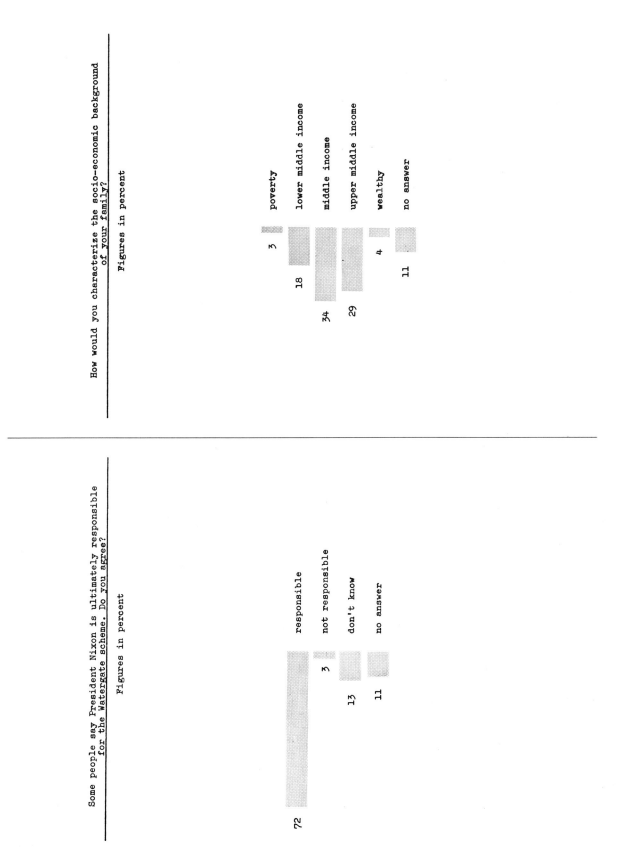

How would you characterize the socio-economic background
of your family?

Figures in percent

3 — poverty

18 — lower middle income

34 — middle income

29 — upper middle income

4 — wealthy

11 — no answer

Some people say President Nixon is ultimately responsible
for the Watergate scheme. Do you agree?

Figures in percent

72 — responsible

3 — not responsible

13 — don't know

11 — no answer

Do you think the preferences of those who financially back the
art world influence the kind of work artists produce?

Figures in percent

yes, a lot 30

somewhat 37

slightly 10

not at all 9

don't know 2

no answer 12

What is the religious background of your family?

Figures in percent

Catholic 18

Protestant 26

Jewish 28

other 3

mixed 10

none 7

no answer 9

It has been charged that the present U.S. Government is catering to business interests. Do you think this is the case?

Figures in percent

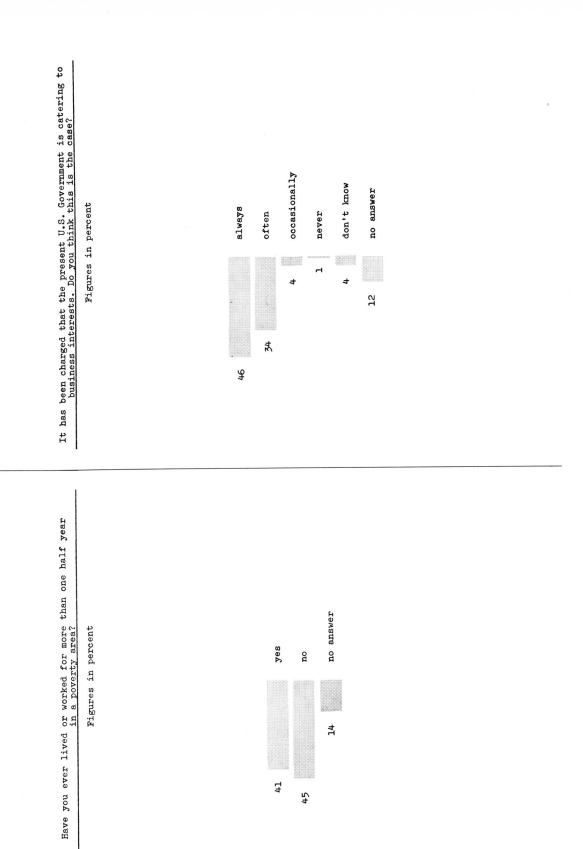

always   46

often   34

occasionally   4

never   1

don't know   4

no answer   12

Have you ever lived or worked for more than one half year in a poverty area?

Figures in percent

yes   41

no   45

no answer   14

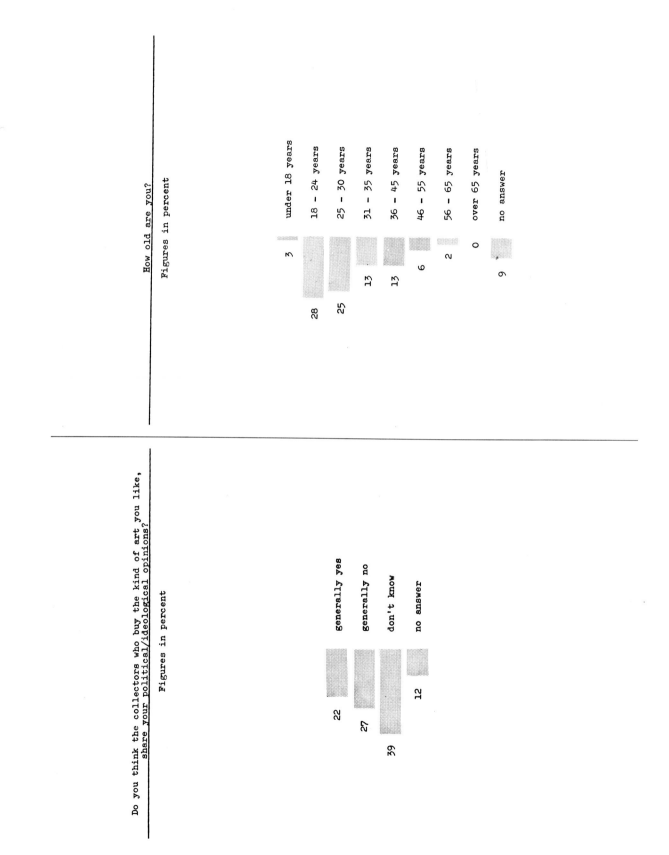

How old are you?

Figures in percent

under 18 years	3
18 - 24 years	28
25 - 30 years	25
31 - 35 years	13
36 - 45 years	13
46 - 55 years	6
56 - 65 years	2
over 65 years	0
no answer	9

Do you think the collectors who buy the kind of art you like, share your political/ideological opinions?

Figures in percent

generally yes	22
generally no	27
don't know	39
no answer	12

50

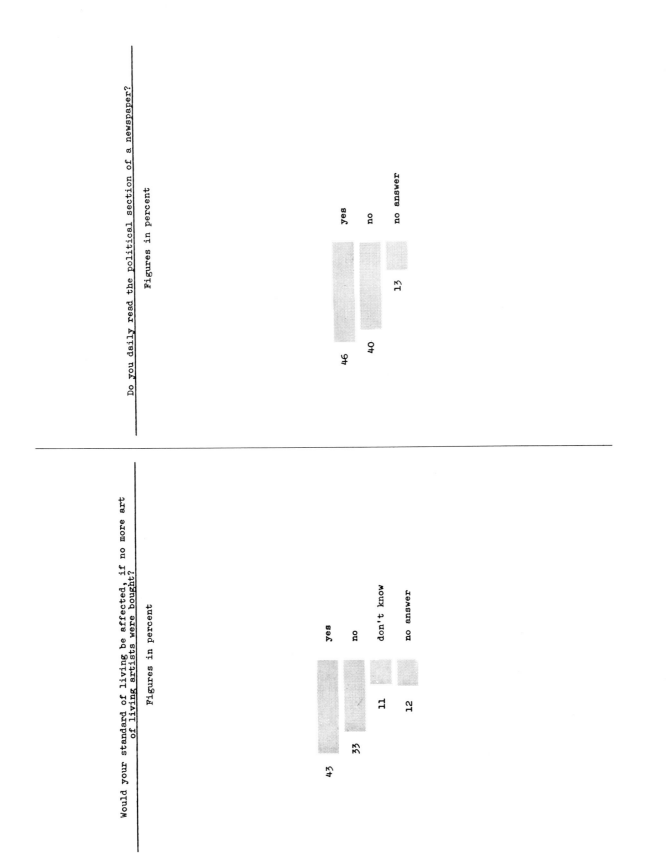

Would your standard of living be affected, if no more art of living artists were bought?

Figures in percent

yes 43

no 33

don't know 11

no answer 12

Do you daily read the political section of a newspaper?

Figures in percent

yes 46

no 40

no answer 13

Do you think the visitors of the J. Weber Gallery who participated
in the poll differed from those who did not?

Figures in percent

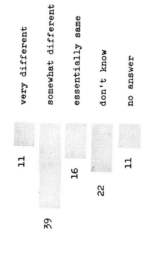

very different   11

somewhat different   39

essentially same   16

don't know   22

no answer   11

Do you think the preferences of those who financially back the art
world influence the kind of work artists produce?

Graphs compare relative distribution of opinions to above question,
in percent, within each group of responses to bottom question.

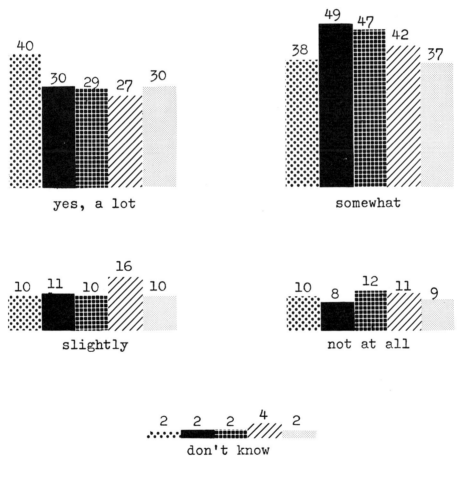

yes, a lot   somewhat

slightly   not at all

don't know

Do you have a professional interest in art?

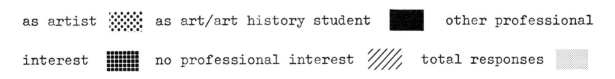

as artist ⠿   as art/art history student ▮   other professional

interest ▦   no professional interest ⧄   total responses ▨

Do you think the preferences of those who financially back the art
world influence the kind of work artists produce?

Graphs compare relative distribution of opinions to above question,
in percent, within each group of responses to bottom question.

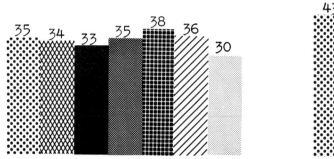

yes, a lot

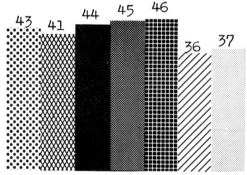

somewhat

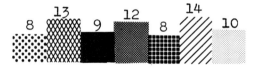

slightly

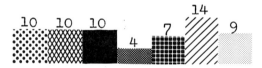

not at all

don't know

How much money have you spent on buying art (total)?

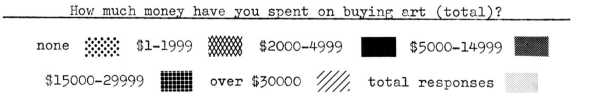

none $1-1999 $2000-4999 $5000-14999

$15000-29999   over $30000   total responses

Do you think the preferences of those who financially back the art
world influence the kind of work artists produce?

Graphs compare relative distribution of opinions to above question,
in percent, within each group of responses to bottom question.

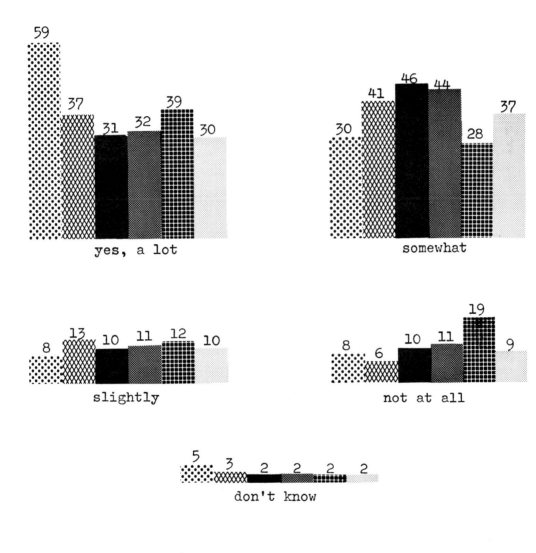

yes, a lot

somewhat

slightly

not at all

don't know

How would you characterize the socio-economic status of your parents?

poverty   lower middle income   middle income

upper middle income   wealthy   total responses

Do you think the preferences of those who financially back the art world influence the kind of work artists produce?

Graphs compare relative distribution of opinions to above question, in percent, within each group of responses to bottom question.

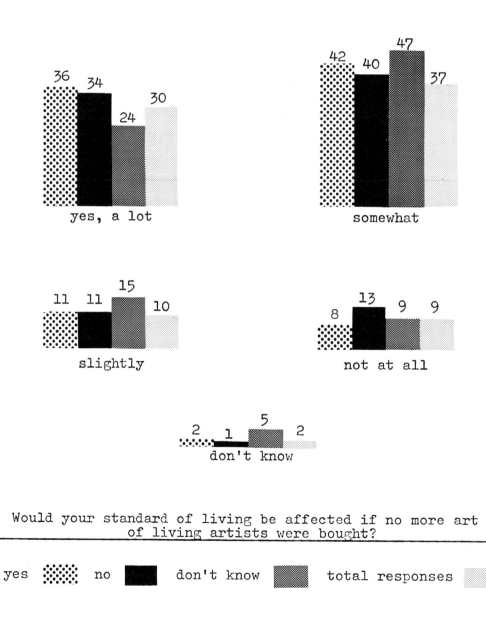

Would your standard of living be affected if no more art of living artists were bought?

yes ▨   no ■   don't know ▨   total responses ▨

Do you think the preferences of those who financially back the art
world influence the kind of work artists produce?

Graphs compare relative distribution of opinions to above question,
in percent, within each group of responses to bottom question.

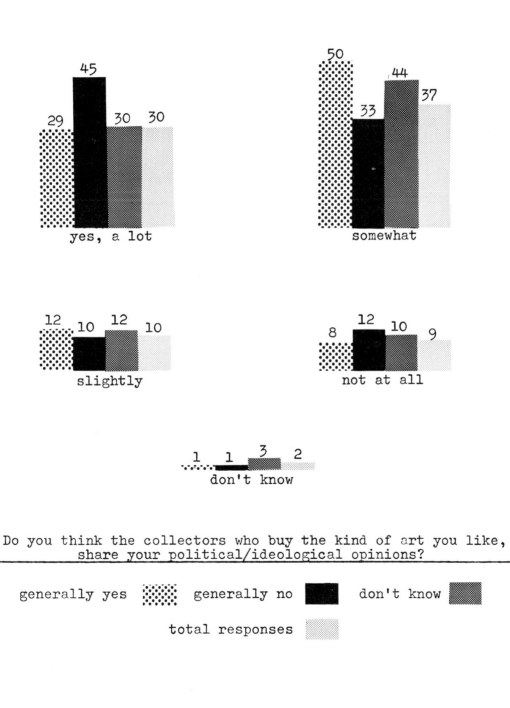

Do you think the collectors who buy the kind of art you like,
share your political/ideological opinions?

generally yes   generally no   don't know

total responses

Do you think the preferences of those who financially back the art
world influence the kind of work artists produce?

Graphs compare relative distribution of opinions to above question,
in percent, within each group of responses to bottom question.

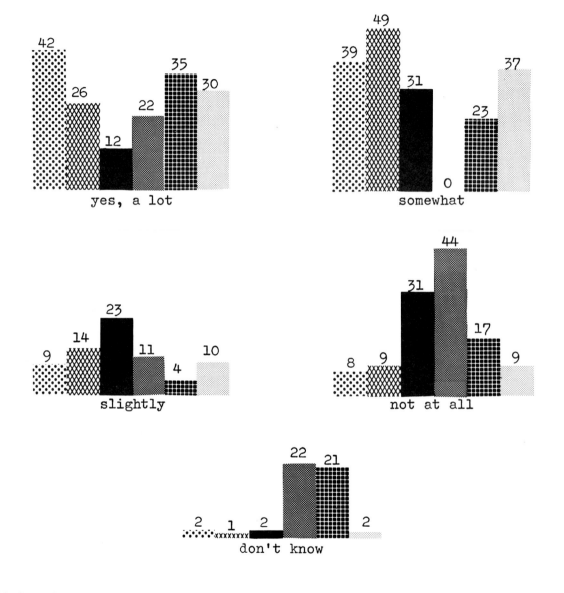

yes, a lot

somewhat

slightly

not at all

don't know

It has been charged that the present U.S. Government is catering to
business interests. Do you think this is the case?

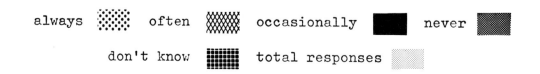

always   often   occasionally   never

don't know   total responses

58

Solomon R. Guggenheim Museum
Board of Trustees

Solomon R. Guggenheim Museum Board of Trustees

1974. 7 panels, 20″ × 24″ (50.8 × 61 cm), under glass, framed in brass.

First exhibited in group show, *Live!*, with Allan Kaprow, Les Levine, Dennis Oppenheim, at Stefanotty Gallery, New York, March 1974.

Coll. Dr. Herman J. Daled, Chef de Département Honoraire at the Clinique Universitaire de Radiologie, Brussels, Belgium.

SOLOMON R. GUGGENHEIM MUSEUM

GUGGENHEIM FAMILY MEMBERS AMONG TRUSTEES

SOLOMON R. GUGGENHEIM MUSEUM

CORPORATE AFFILIATION OF TRUSTEES

Kennecott Copper Corporation

FRANK R. MILLIKEN, President, Chief Exec. Officer & Member Board of Directors

PETER O. LAWSON-JOHNSTON, Member Board of Directors

ALBERT E. THIELE, past Member Board of Directors

Multinational company mining, smelting, refining copper, molybdenum, gold, zinc and coal. Copper based mill products.

Operates in the U.S., Australia, Brazil, Canada, Colombia, Costa Rica, England, Indonesia, Italy, Netherlands Antilles, Nigeria, Peru, South Africa.

El Teniente, Kennecott's Chilean copper mine, was nationalized July, 1971 through Constitutional Reform Law, passed unanimously by Chilean Congress. Chilean Comptroller General ruled profits over 12% a year since 1955 to be considered excess and deducted from compensation. His figures, disputed by Kennecott, in effect, eliminated any payments.

Kennecott tried to have Chilean copper shipments confiscated or customers payments attached. Although without ultimate success in European courts, legal harassment threatened Chilean economy (copper 70% of export).

President Salvador Allende addressed United Nations December 4, 1972. The New York Times reported:

The Chilean President had still harsher words for two U.S. companies, the International Telephone & Telegraph Corp. and the Kennecott Corp., which he said, had "dug their claws into my country", and which proposed "to manage our political life."

Dr. Allende said that from 1955 to 1970 the Kennecott Copper Corp. had made an average profit of 52.8% on its investments.

He said that huge "transnational" corporations were waging war against sovereign states and that they were "not accountable to or representing the collective interest."

In a statement issued in reply to Dr. Allende's charges, Frank R. Milliken, president of Kennecott, referred to legal actions now being taken by his company in courts overseas to prevent the Chilean Government from selling copper from the nationalized mines:

"No amount of rhetoric can alter the fact that Kennecott has been a responsible corporate citizen of Chile for more than 50 years and has made substantial contributions to both the economic and social well-being of the Chilean people."

"Chile's expropriation of Kennecott's property without compensation violates established principles of international law. We will continue to pursue any legal remedies that may protect our shareholders' equity."

President Allende died in a military coup Sept. 11, 1973. The Junta committed itself to compensate Kennecott for nationalized property.

1973   Net sales : $1,425,613,531   Net after taxes : $159,363,059   Earn. per com. share : $4.81

29,100 employees

Office: 161 E. 42 St., New York, N.Y.

SOLOMON R. GUGGENHEIM MUSEUM

CORPORATE AFFILIATION OF TRUSTEES

Pacific Tin Consolidated Corporation

PETER O. LAWSON-JOHNSTON, Vice Chairman & Member Board of Directors

ALBERT E. THIELE, Member Board of Directors

A. CHAUNCEY NEWLIN, past Member Board of Directors

(F. Stuart Miller, Chairman & Member Board of Directors of Pacific Tin Consolidated Corp. is a partner of P.O. Lawson-Johnston and A.E. Thiele in Guggenheim Brothers firm)

Mining and processing tin, feldspar, diamonds

Operations in the United States, Malaysia, Brazil

Investment in Companhia de Diamantes de Angola

Sales range $9-12 million. 800 employees

Office: 120 Broadway, New York, N.Y.

Feldspar Corporation
Subsidiary of Pacific Tin Consolidated Corp.

PETER O. LAWSON-JOHNSTON, Chairman & Member Board of Directors

(F. Stuart Miller, Member Board of Directors of Feldspar Corp., is a partner of P.O. Lawson-Johnston in Guggenheim Brothers firm)

Products: Feldspar, mica, silica sand

Sales range $3-6 million. 280 employees

Office: 120 Broadway, New York, N.Y.

Companhia de Diamantes de Angola

ALBERT E. THIELE, Member Board of Directors

Diamond mining with investment of Pacific Tin Consolidated Corp.

Manet-PROJEKT '74

Manet-PROJEKT '74

1974. 10 panels, 20½" × 31½" (52 × 80 cm), and one color reproduction of Manet's *Bunch of Asparagus,* size of original plus frame, 32¾" × 37" (83 × 94 cm), all in thin black frames under glass. Color reproduction: Fotofachlabor Rolf Lillig, Cologne.

First exhibited Paul Maenz Gallery, Cologne, July 1974.

Coll. Prof. Dr. med. Roger Matthys, Werkleider at the Rijksuniversiteit, Kliniek Maria Middelares, Deurle, Belgium.

PROJEKT '74 was an exhibition billed to present "aspects of international art at the beginning of the seventies". It was staged in the summer of 1974 by the Cologne Wallraf-Richartz-Museum, on the occasion of its 150th anniversary and at a cost of more than $300,000. It was advertised with the slogan, "Art Remains Art". The Cologne Kunsthalle, like the Museum a City institution, and the local Kunstverein, a private institution with subsidies from the City, joined the Wallraf-Richartz-Museum in this exhibition.

Invited to participate in the show, I submitted a general outline for my work, which read:

> Manet's "Bunch of Asparagus" of 1880, collection Wallraf-Richartz-Museum, is on a studio easel in an approx. 6 × 8 meter room of PROJEKT '74. Panels on the walls present the social and economic position of the persons who have owned the painting over the years and the prices paid for it.

Dr. Evelyn Weiss, the modern art curator of the Wallraf-Richartz-Museum and one of the six members of the PROJEKT '74 organizing team, responded that this plan was "one of the best projects submitted", but that it could not be executed in the exhibition nor printed in the catalogue.

This decision was reached in what was described as a "democratic vote" by the organizing team. The vote was 3:3. Voting for the work's exhibition were Dr. Evelyn Weiss, Dr. Manfred Schneckenburger, director of the Kunsthalle and Dr. Wulf Herzogenrath, director of the Kunstverein. The votes against the work were cast by Dr. Horst Keller, director of the Wallraf-Richartz-Museum, Dr. Albert Schug, the Museum's librarian, and by Dr. Dieter Ronte, the personal aide of Prof. Dr. Gert von der Osten, who was head of all Cologne municipal museums and co-director of the Wallraf-Richartz-Museum until his retirement in 1975. With the exception of the director of the private Kunstverein, all team members were subordinates of Prof. von der Osten.

In this vote, the artistic qualification of my work was not in question nor were technical difficulties an issue. It was to be decided if one was to follow Dr. Keller's considerations which he explained to me in a letter of May 8.

Dr. Keller objected to my listing Hermann J. Abs' 19 positions on boards of directors. I portrayed his social and economic standing because, in his capacity as chairman, he represented the Wallraf-Richartz-Kuratorium (Association of the Friends of the Museum), when it acquired the Manet painting. After explaining that the Museum, although financially carried by the City and the State (province), depends on private donations for major acquisitions, he continued:

> It would mean giving an absolutely inadequate evaluation of the spiritual initiative of a man if one were to relate in any way the host of offices he holds in totally different walks of life with such an idealistic

engagement . . . A grateful museum, however, and a grateful city or one ready to be moved to gratefulness must protect initiatives of such an extraordinary character from any other interpretation which might later throw even the slightest shadow on it . . .

Responding to correspondence from me, he maintained his position in a second letter and remarked, "A museum knows nothing about economic power; it does indeed, however, know something about spiritual power."

Dr. Keller and Prof. von der Osten never saw or showed any interest in seeing my work before they rejected it. On July 4, the day of the press opening of PROJEKT '74, it went on exhibition, instead, at the Paul Maenz Gallery in Cologne, with a 1:1 color reproduction in place of the original "Bunch of Asparagus".

Daniel Buren, participating in PROJEKT '74, incorporated a scaled-down facsimile of my Manet-PROJEKT '74, which I had provided at his request, in his work at the Kunsthalle. He attached a poster titled, "Art Remains Politics", referring to the exhibition's official slogan, "Art Remains Art", with an excerpt from *Limites Critiques*, an essay he had written in 1970:

   . . . Art whatever it may be is exclusively political. What is called for is the *analysis of formal and cultural limits* (and not one *or* the other) within which art exists and struggles. These limits are many and of different intensities. Although the prevailing ideology and the associated artists try in every way *to camouflage* them, and although it is too early — the conditions are not met — to blow them up, the time has come *to unveil* them.

On the morning after the opening, Prof. von der Osten, without contacting Buren, had those parts of his work, which I had provided, pasted over with double layers of white paper.

A few artists, among them Antonio Diaz, Frank Gilette and Newton and Helen Harrison, temporarily or permanently closed down their works in protest. Carl Andre, Robert Filliou and Sol LeWitt, hearing that my work was not admitted in the exhibition, had previously withdrawn from the show.

In response to a question by Prof. Carl R. Baldwin, who was preparing an article on the incident for *Art in America,* Dr. Keller wrote, in a letter dated Sept. 25, 1974, "In any event, it is a not uncommon practice for a museum to paste over an artist's work, when an artist has expressly disregarded an agreement previously reached with a museum . . ."

"Bunch of Asparagus"
1880 painted by
Edouard Manet

Lived from 1832 to 1883 in Paris. Descendant of a well-to-do Catholic family of the French bourgeoisie. Father Auguste Manet, lawyer, chief of personnel at Ministry of Justice, later judge (magistrat) at the Cour d'appel de Paris (Appelate Court). Republican. Knight of the Legion of Honor. Grandfather Clément Manet, mayor of Gennevilliers on the Seine, near Paris. Family owns 133 acre farm there. Mother Eugénie Desirée Fournier, daughter of French diplomat who managed the election of Marshall Bernadotte to the Swedish throne. Charles XIV of Sweden, her godfather. Her brother, Clément Fournier, colonel in the artillery. Resigned during revolution 1848. Two brothers of Manet in the civil service.

Manet attends renowned Collège Rollin (with Antonin Proust, later politician and writer). Goes to sea for a short while, contrary to his father's wish for law studies. Fails entrance exam for Naval Academy.

1850-56 studies art in private atelier of Thomas Couture, a successful salon painter. Travels to Italy, Germany, Austria, Switzerland, Belgium, Holland, Spain.

Financially independent. Does not depend on the sale of his paintings. Lives in richly furnished Parisian houses, with servants.

Exhibits since 1861 at the Salon and in private art galleries with uneven success. 1863 participation in the "Salon des Refusés" (Salon of the Rejected). Paintings are attacked by official criticism for their offenses against the convention. Support from Zola, Mallarmé, Rimbaud.

Marries Suzanne Leenhoff 1863, after the death of his father. She is his former piano teacher, daughter of a Dutch musician. Her son, Léon Edouard Koëlla, born 1852, is Manet's illegitimate child; adopted by Manet.

1870, in protest against conservative jury, exhibits 50 paintings in a black barrack erected at his own expense for 18,000 francs on the grounds of the Marquis de Pomereu, near the World's Fair in Paris. Followers among younger, especially impressionist artists.

Participates in the defense of Paris as a national guardsman during the Franco-German War 1870. Messenger for the regimental staff. During the Paris Commune with his family in Southern France. Antiroyalist. Admirer of the republican Léon Gambetta, the Prime Minister to be.

1871, the art dealer Durand-Ruel, a friend of impressionist painting, buys a great number of his works. Meets with the approval of circles of the Parisian Society who are open to artistic innovation. Numerous commissions of portraits. Wins 2nd Medal of Salon 1881. At the suggestion of Antonin Proust appointed Knight of the Legion of Honor.

During his fatal illness treated by former physician of Napoleon III.

1883, memorial exhibition at the Ecole des Beaux-Arts, Paris. Preface to catalogue by Emile Zola. Proceeds of sales for heirs 116,637 francs.

Das Spargel-Stilleben

1880 gemalt von

Edouard Manet

Lebt von 1832 bis 1883 in Paris. – Entstammt einer katholischen Familie des franz. Großbürgertums. Vater Auguste Manet Jurist, Personalchef im Justizministerium, später Richter (magistrat) am Cour d'appel de Paris (Berufungsgericht). Republikaner. Ritter der Ehrenlegion. – Großvater Clément Manet Bürgermeister von Gennevilliers an der Seine, vor Paris. Familie besitzt dort ein 54 Hektar großes Landgut. – Mutter Eugénie Désirée Fournier, Tochter eines franz. Diplomaten, der die Wahl Marschall Bernadottes zum schwedischen König betrieb. Karl XIV. von Schweden ihr Pate. – Ihr Bruder Clément Fournier Artillerieoberst. Demissioniert während der Revolution 1848. – Zwei Brüder Manets im Staatsdienst.

Manet besucht renommiertes Collège Rollin (Mitschüler Antonin Proust, späterer Politiker und Schriftsteller). Entgegen dem väterlichen Wunsch nach einem Jurastudium fährt er für kurze Zeit zur See. Fällt bei der Aufnahmeprüfung zur Seekadettenanstalt durch.

1850–56 Kunststudium im Privatatelier von Thomas Couture, einem erfolgreichen Salonmaler. Studienreisen nach Italien, Deutschland, Österreich, der Schweiz, Belgien, Holland, Spanien.

Finanziell unabhängig. Nicht auf den Verkauf seiner Bilder angewiesen. Wohnt in großen standesgemäß eingerichteten Häusern in Paris, mit Dienerschaft.

Stellt ab 1861 mit wechselndem Erfolg im Salon und in Kunsthandlungen aus. 1863 Beteiligung am „Salon des Réfusés" (Salon der Zurückgewiesenen). Bilder werden wegen Verstössen gegen die Konvention von der offiziellen Kritik bekämpft. Kritische Unterstützung durch Zola, Mallarmé, Rimbaud.

Heiratet 1863 nach dem Tod seines Vaters Suzanne Leenhoff, seine ehemalige Klavierlehrerin, die Tochter eines holländischen Musikers. Léon Edouard Koëlla, ihr 1852 geborener Sohn, ist ein illegitimes Kind Manets; wird von ihm adoptiert.

Stellt 1867 aus Protest gegen die konservative Jury 50 Bilder in einer für 18 000 Francs selbstfinanzierten Baracke auf einem Grundstück des Marquis de Pomereu in der Nähe der Weltausstellung in Paris aus. Anhänger unter jüngeren, besonders impressionistischen Künstlern.

Als Nationalgardist 1870 bei der Verteidigung von Paris im Deutsch-Französischen Krieg, Meldegänger im Regimentsstab. Während der Pariser Kommune bei seiner Familie in Südfrankreich. – Antiroyalist. Bewunderer des Republikaners Léon Gambetta, des späteren Ministerpräsidenten.

1871 umfangreiche Bilderkäufe durch den Kunsthändler Durand-Ruel, einem Freund impressionistischer Malerei. Findet Anerkennung in den für künstlerische Neuerungen aufgeschlossenen Kreisen der Pariser Gesellschaft. Zahlreiche Porträtaufträge. 1881 Gewinn der 2. Medaille des Salons. Auf Vorschlag Antonin Prousts Ernennung zum Ritter der Ehrenlegion.

Während seiner tödlichen Krankheit Behandlung durch früheren Leibarzt Napoleon III.

1883 Gedächtnisausstellung in der Ecole des Beaux-Arts Paris. Katalogvorwort von Emile Zola. Verkaufserlös zugunsten der Erben 116 637 Francs.

"Bunch of Asparagus"
1880 for 800 francs acquired by
Charles Ephrussi

Born 1849 in Odessa, dies 1905 in Paris. Descendant of Jewish family of bankers with banks in Odessa, Vienna, Paris. Family relations to French high finance (Baron de Reinach, Baron de Rothschild).

Studies in Odessa and Vienna. 1871, moves to Paris.

Own banking activities. Art historical writings about Albrecht Dürer, Jacopo de Barbarij and Paul Baudry, etc., 1875, works for "Gazette des Beaux-Arts," 1885, co-owner, 1894, publisher.

Member of numerous cultural committees and salons of Parisian Society. With Gustave Dreyfus, the Comtesse Greffulhe and Princess Mathilde organization of art exhibitions and concerts of the works of Richard Wagner, among others. Second model for Marcel Proust's Swann.

Collector of works from the Renaissance, the 18th century, and of Albrecht Dürer, East Asian Art and contemporary painters.

Instead of paying Manet 800 francs, for "Bunch of Asparagus" as agreed upon, he pays 1000 francs. To show his gratitude Manet sends him the still life of a single asparagus (1880, oil on canvas, 6½ × 8½", Paris, Musée de l'Impressionisme) with a note: "There is one still missing in your bunch."

Knight (1881), Officer (1903) in the Legion of Honor.

Engraving by M. Patricot, "Charles Ephrussi", from "La Gazette des Beaux-Arts", Paris, 1905

Das Spargel-Stilleben

1880 für 800 Francs gekauft durch

Charles Ephrussi

Geboren 1849 in Odessa, gestorben 1905 in Paris. – Entstammt jüdischer Bankiersfamilie mit Bankunternehmen in Odessa, Wien und Paris. Familiäre Beziehungen zur franz. Hochfinanz (Baron de Reinach, Baron de Rothschild).

Studiert in Odessa und Wien. – 1871 Übersiedlung nach Paris.

Eigene Bankgeschäfte. – Kunstschriftstellerische Arbeiten u. a. über Albrecht Dürer, Jacopo de Barbarij und Paul Baudry. 1875 Mitarbeit an der „Gazette des Beaux Arts", 1885 Mitinhaber, 1894 Herausgeber.

Mitglied zahlreicher kultureller Komitees und Salons der Pariser Gesellschaft. Organisiert mit Gustave Dreyfus, der Comtesse Greffulhe und der Prinzessin Mathilde Kunstausstellungen und Konzerte, u. a. von Werken Richard Wagners. – Zweites Vorbild für Marcel Prousts Swann.

Sammelt Kunst der Renaissance, des 18. Jahrhunderts, Albrecht Dürers, Ostasiatische Kunst und Werke zeitgenössischer Maler.

Zahlt Manet statt der vereinbarten 800 Francs für das „Spargel-Stilleben" insgesamt 1000 Francs. Aus Dankbarkeit schickt im Manet das Stilleben eines einzelnen Spargels (1880, Öl auf Leinwand, 16,5 x 21,5 cm, Paris Musée de l'Impressionisme) mit der Bemerkung : „Es fehlte noch in Ihrem Bündel".

Ritter (1882) und Offizier (1903) der Ehrenlegion.

Gravure von M. Patricot „Charles Ephrussi" aus „La Gazette des Beaux Arts", Paris 1905

"Bunch of Asparagus"
between 1900 and 1902 acquired by
Alexandre Rosenberg

Born about 1850 in Pressburg (Bratislava), dies 1913 in Paris. Descendant of a Jewish family from Bohemia.

Immigrates to Paris at the age of nine.

1870, founds a firm dealing with antiques and fine art.

1878, marries Mathilde Jellineck of a Viennese family. They have three sons and one daughter.

After his death in 1913, continuation of the firm by his youngest son, Paul, born 1881 in Paris. Specialization in the art of the 19th and 20th century. 1940, moves to New York. At present, Paul Rosenberg & Co. in New York, headed by Alexandre Rosenberg, a grandson.

Charlot, charcoal, "Portrait of Alexandre Rosenberg".

Das Spargel-Stilleben

zwischen 1900 und 1902 gekauft durch

Alexandre Rosenberg

Geboren um 1850 in Preßburg (Bratislava), Slovakei. – Entstammt jüdischer Familie. Emigration nach Paris im Alter von 9 Jahren.

1870 Gründung einer Kunst- und Antiquitätenhandlung in Paris.

Heiratet 1878 Mathilde Jellineck aus Wien. Sie haben drei Söhne und eine Tochter.

Fortführung der Firma nach seinem Tode 1913 durch den 1881 in Paris geborenen Sohn Paul Rosenberg. Spezialisierung auf die Kunst des 19. und 20. Jahrhunderts. – Gegenwärtig Paul Rosenberg & Co. in New York, geführt durch den Enkel Alexandre Rosenberg.

Kohlezeichnung von Louis Charlot „Alexandre Rosenberg" (Ausschnitt), 1913.

"Bunch of Asparagus"
as of unknown date owned by or on consignment with
Paul Cassirer

Born 1871 in Görlitz, suicide 1926 in Berlin. Descendant of well-to-do Jewish family. Father, Louis Cassirer; with 2 sons, founder of firm Dr. Paul Cassirer & Co., Kabelwerke (cable factory) in Berlin. Brother, Prof. Richard Cassirer, neurologist in Berlin. Cousin, Prof. Ernst Cassirer, renowned philosopher.

Studies art history in Munich. One of the editors of "Simplizissimus". Own writings.

1898, with his cousin, Bruno Cassirer, founder of publishing house and art gallery in Berlin. 1901, partnership dissolved. Continues Kunstsalon Paul Cassirer (gallery), Victoriastrasse 35, in wealthy section of Berlin.

Opponent, with "Berliner Sezession" (association of artists), of official art of the court. Inspite of the Kaiser's indignation, support of French Impressionism through publications and art-dealing. Close relation to Parisian art dealer Durand-Ruel. Promotes German painters Trübner, Liebermann, Corinth, Slevogt.

1908, founds publishing house, Paul Cassirer, for art publications, fiction, and poetry. Publishes works of literary expressionism. 1910, foundation of bi-monthly magazine "Pan" and Pan-Society for the promotion of dramatic works, among them works by Wedekind.

From first marriage one daughter and one son (suicide during World War I). Second marriage to actress Tilla Durieux.

1914, army volunteer. Awarded Iron Cross at Ypers. Becomes pacifist.

Temporarily imprisoned (accused of having illegally sold French paintings). Escapes to Switzerland and stays in Berne and Zurich until the end of the war. Assists Harry Graf Kessler with French contacts for negotiations with France on behalf of Ludendorff. Publishes pacifist writings with Max Rascher.

After revolution of 1918 in Berlin member of USPD (Leftist faction of Social Democratic Party).

Publishes socialist books by Kautzky and Bernstein, among others.

Motives for suicide, 1926, probably related to conflict with Tilla Durieux.

Continuation of Kunstsalon Paul Cassirer in Amsterdam, Zurich, and London by Dr. Walter Feilchenfeldt and Dr. Grete Ring, a niece of Max Liebermann.

Lithography by Max Oppenheimer, "Portrait of Paul Cassirer", around 1925

Das Spargel-Stilleben
von unbekanntem Datum an im Besitz von oder
in Kommission bei

Paul Cassirer

Geboren 1871 in Görlitz, Selbstmord 1926 in Berlin. – Entstammt wohlhabender jüdischer Familie. Vater Louis Cassirer gründet mit 2 Söhnen die Firma Dr. Cassirer & Co., Kabelwerke in Berlin. – Bruder Prof. Richard Cassirer, Berliner Neurologe. – Vetter Prof. Ernst Cassirer bekannter Philosoph.

Kunstgeschichtsstudium in München. Mitredakteur des „Simplizissimus". Eigene literarische Arbeiten.

Gründet mit Vetter Bruno Cassirer 1898 in Berlin Verlags- und Kunsthandlung. 1901 Trennung. Weiterführung als Kunstsalon Paul Cassirer, Victoriastraße 35, in vornehmer Berliner Gegend.

Mit der Künstlervereinigung „Berliner Sezession" Kampf gegen offizielle Hofkunst. Trotz Unwillen des Kaisers Handel und publizistische Förderung des franz. Impressionismus. Enge Beziehungen zum Pariser Kunsthändler Durand-Ruel. Verhilft den Deutschen Malern Trübner, Liebermann, Corinth und Slevogt zum Erfolg.

1908 Gündung des Verlags Paul Cassirer für Kunstliteratur und Belletristik. Publikationen des literarischen Expressionismus. 1910 Gründung der Halbmonatsschrift „Pan" und „Pan"-Gesellschaft zur Förderung von Bühnenwerken, u. a. Wedekind.

Aus erster Ehe eine Tochter und ein Sohn (Selbstmord im 1. Weltkrieg). Heiratet 1910 in zweiter Ehe die Schauspielerin Tilla Durieux.

1914 Kriegsfreiwilliger. Erhält Eisernes Kreuz in Ypern. Wird Kriegsgegner.

Zeitweilig in Haft (beschuldigt, unrechtmäßig franz. Bilder verkauft zu haben). Flucht in die Schweiz und Aufenthalt in Bern und Zürich bis Kriegsende. Verhilft Harry Graf Keßler zu franz. Kontakten für Verhandlungen mit Frankreich im Auftrage Ludendorffs. Verlegt mit Max Rascher pazifistische Literatur.

Nach der Revolution 1918 in Berlin Eintritt in die USPD. Verlegt sozialistische Bücher, u. a. von Kautzky und Bernstein.

Grund für Selbstmord 1926 vermutlich Konflikt mit Tilla Durieux.

Weiterführung des Kunstsalons Paul Cassirer in Amsterdam, Zürich und London durch Dr. Walter Feilchenfeldt und Dr. Grete Ring, eine Nichte Max Liebermanns.

Lithographie von Max Oppenheimer, „Bildnis Paul Cassirer", um 1925.

"Bunch of Asparagus"
for Reichsmark 24,300.—acquired by
Max Liebermann

Painter. 1847 to 1935 lives in Berlin. Descendant of a Jewish family of industrialists. Father, Louis Liebermann, textile industrialist in Berlin. Also owns Eisengiesserei Wilhelmshütte (iron casting plant) in Sprottau, Silesia. Mother, Philipine Haller, daughter of Berlin Jeweller (founder of firm Haller & Rathenau). Brother, Felix Liebermann, well-known historian. Cousin, Walther Rathenau, industrialist (AEG), Foreign Minister of German Reich (murdered 1922).

Liebermann attends renowned Friedrich-Werdersches Gymnasium in Berlin together with sons of Bismarck. Art studies in private Atelier Steffeck, Berlin and at the Art Academy of Weimar. Works several years in Paris, Holland, Munich. Voluntary medic during Franco-German War 1870/71.

Marries Martha Marckwald 1884. Moves back to Berlin. 1885, birth of daughter Käthe Liebermann.

Inherits father's mansion at Pariser Platz 7 (Brandenburg Gate) 1894. Builds summer residence at Wannsee, Grosse Seestrasse 27 (since 1971 Clubhouse of Deutscher Unterwasserclub e.V.) Financially independent of the sale of his works.

1897, major one-man exhibition at the Berliner Akademie der Künste. Great Gold Medal. His paintings, influenced by realism and French impressionism, indignantly rejected by Kaiser Wilhelm II. Paints genre-scenes, urban landscapes, beach-and garden scenes, society portraits, artists, scientists, politicians. Exhibition and sale through Kunstsalon Paul Cassirer in Berlin. Works in public collections, e.g. Wallraf-Richartz-Museum, Cologne.

Awarded honorary title of Professor, 1897. President of the "Berliner Sezession" (association of artists against art of the Kaiser's court) 1898-1911, resignation due to opposition from younger artists. Member (1898), in the Senate (1912), President of the Prussian Academy of Arts, 1920. Resignation, 1933. Honorary doctorate University Berlin. Honorary Citizen of Berlin. Knight of the French Legion of Honor. Order of Oranje-Nassau. Knight of the German Order pour le mérite and other decorations.

Owns works by Cézanne, Daumier, Degas, Manet, Monet, Renoir. Deposits his collection with Kunsthaus Zurich, 1933.

1933 dismissed from all offices by Nazis. Prohibition to exhibit. Removal of his paintings from public collections.

Dies, 1937, in Berlin. His wife, Martha Liebermann, commits suicide, 1943, to avoid arrest.

Photo around 1930

Das Spargel-Stilleben

für 24 300,– RM gekauft durch

Max Liebermann

Maler, lebt von 1847 bis 1935 in Berlin. – Entstammt einer jüdischen Fabrikantenfamilie. Vater Louis Liebermann Textilindustrieller in Berlin. Besitzt ebenfalls Eisengießerei Wilhelmshütte in Sprottau, Schlesien. – Mutter Philipine Haller, Tochter eines Berliner Juweliers (Gründer der Firma Haller & Rathenau). – Bruder Prof. Felix Liebermann, bekannter Historiker. – Vetter Walther Rathenau, Industrieller (AEG), Reichsaußenminister (1922 ermordet).

Liebermann besucht renommiertes Friedrich-Werdersches Gymnasium in Berlin zusammen mit Söhnen Bismarcks. – Kunststudium im Privatatelier Steffeck, Berlin, und auf der Kunstakademie Weimar. Längere Arbeitsaufenthalte in Paris, Holland, München. – Freiwilliger Krankenpfleger im Deutsch-Französischen Krieg 1870/71.

Heiratet 1884 Martha Marckwald, zieht nach Berlin zurück. 1885 Geburt der Tochter Käthe Liebermann.

Erbt 1894 väterliches Palais am Pariser Platz 7 (Brandenburger Tor). Baut 1910 Sommersitz am Wannsee, Große Seestraße 27 (seit 1971 Clubhaus des Deutschen Unterwasserclubs e.V.). Finanziell unabhängig. Lebt nicht vom Verkauf seiner Werke.

1897 Gesamtausstellung in der Berliner Akademie der Künste. Große Goldene Medaille. Seine durch Realismus und franz. Impressionismus beeinflußten Bilder werden von Wilhelm II. empört abgelehnt. – Malt Genreszenen, Stadtlandschaften, Strand- und Gartenszenen, Gesellschaftsporträts, Künstler, Wissenschaftler, Politiker. – Ausstellung und Verkauf durch Kunstsalon Paul Cassirer in Berlin. Werke in öffentlichen Sammlungen u. a. Wallraf-Richartz-Museum Köln.

Professorentitel 1897. – Präsident der „Berliner Sezession" (Künstlervereinigung gegen Hofkunst) 1898–1911, Rücktritt wegen Opposition jüngerer Künstler. – 1898 Mitglied, 1912 im Senat, 1920 Präsident der Preußischen Akademie der Künste. Rücktritt 1933. – Ehrendoktor der Universität Berlin. Ehrenbürger der Stadt Berlin. Ritter der franz. Ehrenlegion. Orden von Oranje-Nassau. Ritter des Ordens Pour le mérite und andere Auszeichnungen.

Besitzt Werke von Cézanne, Daumier, Degas, Manet, Monet, Renoir. Deponiert seine Sammlung 1933 im Kunsthaus Zürich.

1933 von Nazis aus allen Ämtern entlassen. Ausstellungsverbot. Entfernung seiner Bilder aus öffentlichen Sammlungen.

Stirbt 1935 in Berlin. Frau Martha Liebermann begeht 1943 Selbstmord, um sich drohender Verhaftung zu entziehen.

Photo um 1930

"Bunch of Asparagus"
inherited by
Käthe Riezler

Born, 1885, in Berlin, dies 1951, in New York. Daughter of the painter Max Liebermann and his wife Martha Marckwald.

Marries, 1915, Kurt Riezler (Ph.D.). 1917, birth of their daughter Maria Riezler.

Dr. Kurt Riezler, born 1882 in Munich. Son of a businessman. Classical Greek studies at University Munich. 1905, dissertation: "The Second Book of Pseudo-Aristotelian Economics."

1906, enters Foreign Service in Berlin. Second Secretary, later Minister. Worked in the staff of Chancellor von Bethmann-Hollweg. 1919/20 head of the office of President Friedrich Ebert of the German Reich.

1913, under the pseudonym J. J. Ruedorffer, publication of "Prolegomena for a Theory of Politics", 1914 "Basic Traits of World Politics in the Present". Later publications on the philosophy of history, political theory and aesthetics.

1927, professor, vice president and chairman of the board of Goethe University in Frankfurt on Main.

1933, dismissal by Nazis.

Family moves to Berlin into Max Liebermann's house, Pariser Platz 7. 1935, inherits his art collection, which Liebermann had deposited with the Kunsthaus Zürich for protection.

1938, emigration of family to New York. Collection follows.

1939, Dr. Kurt Riezler becomes professor of philosophy at the New School for Social Research in New York, a university founded by emigrants. Visiting professor at the University of Chicago and Columbia University in New York.

Käthe Riezler dies 1951. Dr. Riezler retires 1952, dies in Munich, 1956.

Pastell by Max Liebermann, "The Artist's Daughter", 1901

Das Spargel-Stilleben

vererbt an

Käthe Riezler

Geboren 1885 in Berlin, gestorben 1951 in New York.

Tochter des Malers Max Liebermann und seiner Frau Martha Marckwald.

Heiratet 1915 in Berlin Dr. phil. Kurt Riezler. 1917 Geburt der Tochter Maria Riezler.

Dr. Kurt Riezler, geboren 1882 in München, Sohn eines Kaufmanns. Studium der Klassischen Antike an der Universität München. 1905 Dissertation: „Das zweite Buch der pseudoaristotelischen Ökonomie"

1906 Eintritt ins Auswärtige Amt in Berlin. Legationsrat, später Gesandter. Arbeitet im Stab des Reichskanzlers von Bethmann-Hollweg. 1919/20 Leiter des Büros des Reichspräsidenten Friedrich Ebert.

1913 unter dem Decknamen J. J. Ruedorffer Veröffentlichung der „Prolegomena zu einer Theorie der Politik", 1914 „Grundzüge der Weltpolitik in der Gegenwart". – Später Publikationen zur Geschichtsphilosophie, zur politischen Theorie und Ästhetik.

1927 Honorarprofessor, stellvertretender Geschäftsführer und Vorsitzender des Kuratoriums an der Goethe Universität in Frankfurt am Main.

1933 Entlassung durch Nazis.

Umzug der Familie nach Berlin in das Haus Max Liebermanns, Pariser Platz 7. – Erben 1935 seine Kunstsammlung, die Liebermann 1933 dem Kunsthaus Zürich in Obhut gegeben hatte.

1938 Emigration der Familie nach New York. Sammlung folgt dorthin.

1939 erhält Dr. Riezler eine Professur für Philosophie an der New School for Social Research in New York, einer von Emigranten gegründeten Universität. Gastprofessuren an der University of Chicago und der Columbia University in New York.

Käthe Riezler stirbt 1951. Dr. Riezler emeritiert 1952, stirbt in München 1956.

Pastell von Max Liebermann, „Die Tochter des Künstlers" 1901

"Bunch of Asparagus"
inherited by
Maria White

Born, 1917, in Berlin. Daughter of Prof. Dr. Kurt Riezler and Käthe Liebermann.

Emigrates with her parents to New York in 1938.

Marries Howard Burton White.

Howard B. White, born 1912 in Montclair, N.J. Studies 1934-38 at the New School for Social Research in New York, where Dr. Kurt Riezler teaches. 1941, Rockefeller fellowship. Ph.D. Science, 1943, from New School.

Teaches at Lehigh University and Coe College. At Present Professor for Political and Social Science on the Graduate Faculty of the New School for Social Research. Teaches political philosophy.

Publications: "Peace Among the Willows—The Political Philosophy of Francis Bacon", The Hague 1968; "Copp'd Hills Towards Heaven—Shakespeare and the Classical Polity", The Hague, 1968, among others.

Maria and Howard B. White live in Northport, N.Y. They have two children.

Oil on canvas by Max Liebermann, "The Artist's Daughter and Granddaughter" (Maria Riezler on the right), around 1930

Das Spargel-Stilleben

vererbt an

Maria White

Geboren 1917 in Berlin. – Tochter von Prof. Dr. Kurt Riezler und Käthe Liebermann.

Emigriert 1938 mit ihren Eltern nach New York.

Heiratet Howard Burton White.

Howard B. White, geboren 1912 in Montclair, N. J., studiert 1934–38 an der New School for Social Research in New York, wo Dr. Kurt Riezler lehrt. 1941 Rockefeller Stipendium. Promoviert 1943 an der New School zum Doctor of Science.

Unterrichtet an der Lehigh University und am Coe College. Gegenwärtig Professor im Graduate Department of Political and Social Science der New School for Social Research. Lehrt Political Philosophy.

Veröffentlichungen u. a. „Peace Among the Willows – The Political Philosophy of Francis Bacon", den Haag 1968. „Copp'd Hills Towards Heaven – Shakespeare and the Classical Polity,"den Haag 1968.

Maria und Howard B. White leben in Northport, N. Y. Sie haben zwei Kinder.

Ölbild von Max Liebermann „Tochter und Enkelin des Künstlers" (Maria Riezler im Bild rechts), um 1930

"Bunch of Asparagus"
1968, by way of Mrs. Marianne Feilchenfeldt, Zurich,
for 1,360,000 Deutsch Mark ($260,000) acquired by the

Wallraf-Richartz-Kuratorium and the City of Cologne

Handed over to the Wallraf-Richartz-Museum as a permanent loan by Hermann J. Abs, chairman of the Kuratorium (friends of the Museum), on April 18, 1968, in memory of Konrad Adenauer.

Wallraf-Richartz-Kuratorium und Förderer-Gesellschaft e.V.

Executive Committee and trustees:

Hermann J. Abs, Prof. Dr. Kurt Hansen, Dr. Dr. Günter Henle, Prof. Dr. Ernst Schneider, Prof. Dr. Otto H. Förster, Prof. Dr. Gert von der Osten (managing director)

Trustees: Prof. Dr. Viktor Achter, Dr. Max Adenauer, Fritz Berg, Dr. Walther Berndorff, Theo Burauen, Prof. Dr. Fritz Burgbacher, Dr. Fritz Butschkau, Dr. Felix Eckhardt, Mrs. Gisela Fitting, Prof. Dr. Kurt Forberg, Walter Franz, Dr. Hans Gerling, Dr. Herbert Girardet, Dr. Paul Gülker, Iwan D. Herstatt, Raymund Jörg, Eugen Gottlieb von Langen, Viktor Langen, Dr. Peter Ludwig, Prof. Dr. Heinz Mohnen, Cai Graf zu Rantzau, Karl Gustav Ratjen, Dr. Hans Reuter, Dr. Hans-Günther Sohl, Dr. Werner Schulz, Dr. Nikolaus Graf Strasoldo, Christoph Vowinckel, Otto Wolff von Amerongen

---

Hermann J. Abs handing over the painting.

Das Spargel-Stilleben
1968 über Frau Marianne Feilchenfeldt, Zürich
für 1 360 000,- DM erworben durch das

Wallraf-Richartz-Kuratorium und die Stadt Köln

Dem Wallraf-Richartz-Museum von Hermann J. Abs, dem Vorsitzenden des Kuratoriums, am 18. April 1968 im Andenken an Konrad Adenauer als Dauerleihgabe übergeben.

Das Wallraf-Richartz-Kuratorium und Förderer-Gesellschaft e. V.

Vorstand

Hermann J. Abs
Prof. Dr. Kurt Hansen
Dr. Dr. Günter Henle
Prof. Dr. Ernst Schneider
Prof. Dr. Otto H. Förster
Prof. Dr. Gert von der Osten (geschäftsführend)

Kuratorium

Prof. Dr. Viktor Achter
Dr. Max Adenauer
Fritz Berg
Dr. Walther Berndorff
Theo Burauen
Prof. Dr. Fritz Burgbacher
Dr. Fritz Butschkau
Dr. Felix Eckhardt
Frau Gisela Fitting
Prof. Dr. Kurt Forberg
Walter Franz
Dr. Hans Gerling
Dr. Herbert Girardet
Dr. Paul Gülker
Iwan D. Herstatt
Raymund Jörg
Eugen Gottlieb von Langen
Viktor Langen
Dr. Peter Ludwig
Prof. Dr. Heinz Mohnen
Cai Graf zu.Rantzau
Karl Gustav Ratjen
Dr. Hans Reuter
Dr. Hans-Günther Sohl
Dr. Dr. Werner Schulz
Dr. Nikolaus Graf Strasoldo
Christoph Vowinckel
Otto Wolff von Amerongen

Hermann J. Abs bei der Übergabe des Bildes

"Bunch of Asparagus"
acquired through the initiative of the
Chairman of the Wallraf-Richartz-Kuratorium (Friends of the Museum)
Hermann J. Abs.

Born Bonn 1901. Descendant of a well-to-do Catholic family. Father, Dr. Josef Abs, attorney and Justizrat, co-owner of Hubertus Braunkohlen AG., Brüggen, Erft (brown coal mining company). Mother, Katharina Lückerath.

Passes final exam, 1919, at Realgymnasium Bonn. Studies one semester law, University of Bonn. Bank training at Bankhaus Delbrück von der Heydt & Co., Cologne. Gains experience in international banking in Amsterdam, London, Paris, U.S.A.

Marries Inez Schnitzler 1928. Her father related to Georg von Schnitzler of Executive Committee of I.G. Farben syndicate. Aunt married to Baron Alfred Neven du Mont. Sister married to Georg Graf von der Goltz. Birth of two children, Thomas and Marion Abs.

Member of Zentrumspartei (Catholic Party). 1929, on the staff, with power of attorney, of Bankhaus Delbrück, Schickler & Co., Berlin. 1935-37, one of 5 partners of the Bank.

1937, on the Board of Directors and member of the executive committee of the Deutsche Bank in Berlin. Chief of its foreign division. 1939, appointed member of advisory council of the Deutsche Reichsbank by Walther Funk, Minister of Economics of the Reich. Member of committees of the Reichsbank, Reichsgruppe Industrie, Reichsgruppe Banken, Reichswirtschaftskammer and Arbeitskreis of the Ministry of Economics. 1944, represented on over 50 Boards of Directors. Membership in associations for the advancement of German economic interests abroad.

1946, for 6 weeks in British prison. Cleared by Allied denazification board and placed in category 5 (exonerated of active support of Nazi regime).

1948, participated in foundation of Kreditanstalt für Wiederaufbau (Credit Institute for Reconstruction). Extensive involvement in economic planning of West German Federal Government. Economic advisor of Chancellor Konrad Adenauer. 1951-53 head of German delegation to London conference to negotiate German war debts. Advisory role during negotiations with Israel at Conference on Jewish Material Claims in The Hague. 1954, member of CDU (Christian Democratic Party).

1952, on Board of Directors of Süddeutsche Bank AG. 1957-67, Speaker of Executive Board of Deutsche Bank AG. Since 1967, Chairman of the Board.

Honorary Chairman of the Board of Directors: Deutsche Überseeische Bank, Hamburg — Pittler Maschinenfabrik AG, Langen (Hesse).

Chairman of the Board of Directors: Dahlbusch Verwaltungs-AG, Gelsenkirchen—Daimler Benz AG, Stuttgart—Untertürkheim—Deutsche Bank AG, Frankfurt—Deutsche Lufthansa AG, Köln—Philipp Holzmann AG, Frankfurt—Phoenix Gummiwerke AG, Hamburg-Harburg—RWE Elektrizitätswerk AG, Essen—Vereinigte Glanzstoff AG, Wuppertal-Elberfeld—Zellstoff-Fabrik Waldhof AG, Mannheim.

Honorary Chairman: Salamander AG, Kornwestheim — Gebr. Stumm GmbH, Brambauer (Westf.) — Süddeutsche Zucker-AG, Mannheim.

Vice Chairman of the Board of Directors: Badische Anilin-und Sodafabrik AG, Ludwigshafen—Siemens AG, Berlin-München.

Member of the Board of Directors: Metallgesellschaft AG, Frankfurt.

President of the Supervisory Board: Kreditanstalt für Wiederaufbau — Deutsche Bundesbahn.

Great Cross of the Order of Merit with Star of the Federal Republic of Germany, Papal Star with the Cross of the Commander, Great Cross of Isabella the Catholic of Spain, Cruzeiro do Sul of Brazil. Knight of the Order of the Holy Sepulcher. Honorary doctorates of the Universities of Göttingen, Sofia, Tokyo and the Wirtschaftshochschule Mannheim.

Lives in Kronberg (Taunus), and on Bentgerhof near Remagen.

Photo from "Current Biography Yearbook 1970," New York

Das Spargel-Stilleben
erworben durch die Initiative des
Vorsitzenden des Wallraf-Richartz-Kuratoriums

Hermann J. Abs

Geboren 1901 in Bonn. – Entstammt wohlhabender katholischer Familie. Vater Dr. Josef Abs, Rechtsanwalt und Justizrat, Mitinhaber der Hubertus Braunkohlen AG. Brüggen, Erft. Mutter Katharina Lückerath.

Abitur 1919 Realgymnasium Bonn. – Ein Sem. Jurastudium Universität Bonn. – Banklehre im Kölner Bankhaus Delbrück von der Heydt & Co. Erwirbt internationale Bankerfahrung in Amsterdam, London, Paris, USA.

Heiratet 1928 Inez Schnitzler. Ihr Vater mit Georg von Schnitzler vom Vorstand des IG. Farben-Konzerns verwandt. Tante verheiratet mit Baron Alfred Neven du Mont. Schwester verheiratet mit Georg Graf von der Goltz. – Geburt der Kinder Thomas und Marion Abs.

Mitglied der Zentrumspartei. – 1929 Prokura im Bankhaus Delbrück, Schickler & Co., Berlin. 1935-37 einer der 5 Teilhaber der Bank.

1937 im Vorstand und Aufsichtsrat der Deutschen Bank, Berlin. Leiter der Auslandsabteilung. – 1939 von Reichswirtschaftsminister Funk in den Beirat der Deutschen Reichsbank berufen. – Mitglied in Ausschüssen der Reichsbank, Reichsgruppe Industrie, Reichsgruppe Banken, Reichswirtschafts-kammer und einem Arbeitskreis im Reichswirtschaftsministerium. – 1944 in über 50 Aufsichts- und Verwaltungsräten großer Unternehmen. Mitgliedschaft in Gesellschaften zur Wahrnehmung deutscher Wirtschaftsinteressen im Ausland.

1946 für 6 Wochen in britischer Haft. – Von der Alliierten Entnazifizierungsbehörde als entlastet (5) eingestuft.

1948 bei der Gründung der Kreditanstalt für Wiederaufbau. Maßgeblich an der Wirtschafts-planung der Bundesregierung beteiligt. Wirtschaftsberater Konrad Adenauers. – Leiter der deutschen Delegation bei der Londoner Schuldenkonferenz 1951-53. Berater bei den Wiedergutmachungsver-handlungen mit Israel in Den Haag. 1954 Mitglied der CDU.

1952 im Aufsichtsrat der Süddeutschen Bank AG. – 1957-67 Vorstandssprecher der Deutschen Bank AG. Seit 1967 Vorsitzender des Aufsichtsrats.

Ehrenvorsitzender des Aufsichtsrats:
Deutsche Überseeische Bank, Hamburg – Pittler Maschinenfabrik AG, Langen (Hessen)
Vorsitzender des Aufsichtsrats:
Dahlbusch Verwaltungs-AG, Gelsenkirchen – Daimler Benz AG, Stuttgart-Untertürkheim –
Deutsche Bank AG, Frankfurt – Deutsche Lufthansa AG, Köln – Philipp Holzmann AG, Frankfurt –
Phoenix Gummiwerke AG, Hamburg-Harburg – RWE Elektrizitätswerk AG, Essen –
Vereinigte Glanzstoff AG, Wuppertal-Elberfeld – Zellstoff-Fabrik Waldhof AG, Mannheim

Ehrenvorsitzender:
Salamander AG, Kornwestheim – Gebr. Stumm GmbH, Brambauer (Westf.) –
Süddeutsche Zucker-AG, Mannheim
Stellvertr. Vors. des Aufsichtsrats:
Badische Anilin- und Sodafabrik AG, Ludwigshafen – Siemens AG, Berlin-München
Mitglied des Aufsichtsrats:
Metallgesellschaft AG, Frankfurt
Präsident des Verwaltungsrats:
Kreditanstalt für Wiederaufbau – Deutsche Bundesbahn

Großes Bundesverdienstkreuz mit Stern, Päpstl. Stern zum Komturkreuz, Großkreuz Isabella die Katholische von Spanien, Cruzeiro do Sul von Brasilien. – Ritter des Ordens vom Heiligen Grabe. – Dr. h.c. der Univ. Göttingen, Sofia, Tokio und der Wirtschaftshochschule Mannheim.

Lebt in Kronberg (Taunus) und auf dem Bentgerhof bei Remagen.

Photo aus Current Biography Yearbook 1970 New York

"Bunch of Asparagus"
acquired with donations from

Hermann J. Abs, Frankfurt; Viktor Achter, Mönchengladbach; Agrippina Rückversicherungs AG., Köln; Allianz Versicherung AG., Köln; Heinrich Auer Mühlenwerke, Köln; Bankhaus Heinz Ansmann, Köln; Bankhaus Delbrück von der Heydt & Co., Köln; Bankhaus Sal. Oppenheim Jr. & Cie., Köln; Bankhaus C. G. Trinkaus, Düsseldorf; Dr. Walter Berndorff, Köln; Firma Felix Böttcher, Köln; Robert Bosch GmbH, Köln; Central Krankenversicherungs AG., Köln; Colonia Versicherungs-Gruppe, Köln; Commerzbank AG., Düsseldorf; Concordia Lebensversicherungs AG., Köln; Daimler Benz AG., Stuttgart-Untertürkheim; Demag AG., Duisburg; Deutsch-Atlantische Telegraphenges., Köln; Deutsche Bank AG., Frankfurt; Deutsche Central-bodenkredit AG., Köln; Deutsche Continental-Gas-Ges., Düsseldorf; Deutsche Krankenversicherungs AG., Köln; Deutsche Libby-Ownes-Ges. AG., Gelsenkirchen; Deutsche Solvay-Werke GmbH, Solingen-Ohligs; Dortmunder Union-Brauerei, Dortmund; Dresdner Bank AG., Düsseldorf; Farbenfabriken Bayer AG., Leverkusen; Gisela Fitting, Köln; Autohaus Jacob Fleischhauer K.G., Köln; Glanzstoff AG., Wuppertal; Graf Rüdiger von der Goltz, Düsseldorf; Dr. Paul Gülker, Köln; Gottfried Hagen AG., Köln; Hein. Lehmann & Co. AG., Düsseldorf; Hilgers AG., Rheinbrohl; Hoesch AG., Dortmund; Helmut Horten GmbH, Düsseldorf; Hubertus Brauerei GmbH, Köln; Karstadt-Peters GmbH, Köln; Kaufhalle GmbH, Köln; Kaufhof AG., Köln; Kleinwanzlebener Saatzucht AG., Einbeck; Klöckner Werke AG., Duisburg; Kölnische Lebens-und Sachvers. AG., Köln; Viktor Langen, Düsseldorf-Meerbusch; Margarine Union AG., Hamburg; Mauser-Werke GmbH, Köln; Josef Mayr K.G., Hagen; Michel Brennstoffhandel GmbH, Düsseldorf; Gert von der Osten, Köln; Kurt Pauli, Lövenich; Pfeifer & Langen, Köln; Preussag AG., Hannover; William Prym Werke AG., Stolberg; Karl-Gustav Ratjen, Königstein (Taunus); Dr. Hans Reuter, Duisburg; Rheinisch-Westf. Bodenkreditbank, Köln; Rhein.-Westf. Isolatorenwerke GmbH, Siegburg; Rhein.-Westf. Kalkwerke AG., Dornap; Sachtleben AG., Köln; Servais-Werke AG., Witterschlick; Siemag Siegener Maschinenbau GmbH, Dahlbruch; Dr. F. E. Shinnar, Tel-Ganim (Israel); Sparkasse der Stadt Köln, Köln; Schlesische Feuervers.-Ges., Köln; Ewald Schneider, Köln; Schoellersche Kammgarnspinnerei AG., Eitorf; Stahlwerke Bochum AG., Bochum; Dr. Josef Steegmann, Köln-Zürich; Strabag Bau AG., Köln; Dr. Nikolaus Graf Strasoldo, Burg Gudenau; Cornelius Stüssgen AG., Köln; August Thyssen-Hütte AG., Düsseldorf; Union Rhein. Braunkohlen AG., Wesseling; Vereinigte Aluminium-Werke AG., Bonn; Vereinigte Glaswerke, Aachen; Volkshilfe Lebensversicherungs AG., Köln; Jos. Voss GmbH & Co. KG., Brühl; Walther & Cie. AG., Köln; Wessel-Werk GmbH, Bonn; Westdeutsche Bodenkreditanstalt, Köln; Westd. Landesbank Girozentrale, Düsseldorf; Westfalenbank AG., Bochum; Rud. Siedersleben'sche O. Wolff-Stiftg., Köln.

Das Spargel-Stilleben
erworben mit Stiftungen von

Hermann J. Abs, Frankfurt
Viktor Achter, Mönchengladbach
Agrippina Rückversicherungs AG., Köln
Allianz Versicherung AG., Köln
Heinrich Auer Mühlenwerke, Köln
Bankhaus Heinz Ansmann, Köln
Bankhaus Delbrück von der Heydt & Co., Köln
Bankhaus Sal. Oppenheim jr. & Cie., Köln
Bankhaus C. G. Trinkaus, Düsseldorf
Dr. Walter Berndorff, Köln
Firma Felix Böttcher, Köln
Robert Bosch GmbH, Köln
Central Krankenversicherungs AG., Köln
Colonia Versicherungs-Gruppe, Köln
Commerzbank AG., Düsseldorf
Concordia Lebensversicherungs AG., Köln
Daimler Benz AG., Stuttgart-Untertürkheim
Demag AG., Duisburg
Deutsch-Atlantische Telegraphenges., Köln
Deutsche Bank AG., Frankfurt
Deutsche Centralbodenkredit AG., Köln
Deutsche Continental-Gas-Ges., Düsseldorf
Deutsche Krankenversicherungs AG., Köln
Deutsche Libby-Owens-Ges. AG., Gelsenkirchen
Deutsche Solvay-Werke GmbH, Solingen-Ohligs
Dortmunder Union-Brauerei, Dortmund
Dresdner Bank AG., Düsseldorf
Farbenfabriken Bayer AG., Leverkusen
Gisela Fitting, Köln
Autohaus Jacob Fleischhauer K. G., Köln
Glanzstoff AG., Wuppertal
Graf Rüdiger von der Goltz, Düsseldorf
Dr. Paul Gülker, Köln
Gottfried Hagen AG., Köln
Hein. Lehmann & Co. AG., Düsseldorf
Hilgers AG., Rheinbrohl
Hoesch AG., Dortmund
Helmut Horten GmbH, Düsseldorf
Hubertus Brauerei GmbH, Köln
Karstadt-Peters GmbH, Köln
Kaufhalle GmbH, Köln
Kaufhof AG, Köln
Kleinwanzlebener Saatzucht AG., Einbeck

Klöckner Werke AG., Duisburg
Kölnische Lebens- und Sachvers. AG., Köln
Viktor Langen, Düsseldorf-Meerbusch
Margarine Union AG., Hamburg
Mauser-Werke GmbH, Köln
Josef Mayr K. G., Hagen
Michel Brennstoffhandel GmbH, Düsseldorf
Gert von der Osten, Köln
Kurt Pauli, Lövenich
Pfeifer & Langen, Köln
Preussag AG., Hannover
William Prym Werke AG., Stolberg
Karl-Gustav Ratjen, Königstein (Taunus)
Dr. Hans Reuter, Duisburg
Rheinisch-Westf. Bodenkreditbank, Köln
Rhein.-Westf. Isolatorenwerke GmbH, Siegburg
Rhein.-Westf. Kalkwerke AG., Dornap
Sachtleben AG., Köln
Servais-Werke AG., Witterschlick
Siemag Siegener Maschinenbau GmbH, Dahlbruch
Dr. F. E. Shinnar, Tel-Ganim (Israel)
Sparkasse der Stadt Köln, Köln
Schlesische Feuervers.-Ges., Köln
Ewald Schneider, Köln
Schoellersche Kammgarnspinnerei AG., Eitorf
Stahlwerke Bochum AG., Bochum
Dr. Josef Steegmann, Köln-Zürich
Strabag Bau AG., Köln
Dr. Nikolaus Graf Strasoldo, Burg Gudenau
Cornelius Stüssgen AG., Köln
August Thyssen-Hütte AG., Düsseldorf
Union Rhein. Braunkohlen AG., Wesseling
Vereinigte Aluminium-Werke AG., Bonn
Vereinigte Glaswerke, Aachen
Volkshilfe Lebensversicherungs AG., Köln
Jos. Voss GmbH & Co. KG., Brühl
Walther & Cie. AG., Köln
Wessel-Werk GmbH, Bonn
Westdeutsche Bodenkreditanstalt, Köln
Westd. Landesbank Girozentrale, Düsseldorf
Westfalenbank AG., Bochum
Rud. Siedersleben'sche O. Wolff-Stiftg., Köln

The gathering of information for this work was assisted by the publications of, or personal communication with:
Hermann J. Abs, Marie Louise Bataille, J. E. Blanche, Geert van Beijeren, Galerie Paul Cassirer, Eberhard Czichon, Théodore Duret, Tilla Durieux, Marianne Feilchenfeldt, Max Friedländer, Hans Graber, Karl Hagemeister, Hancke, Paul Jamot, Annegret Janda, Maurice Jardot, Max Liebermann, Auguste Marguiller, E. Moreau-Nélanton, Max Oppenheimer, Gert von der Osten, Hans Otto A. Ostwald, Jean Patricot, Henri Perruchot, John Rewald, Kurt Riezler, Alexandre Rosenberg, Karl Scheffler, Helmut Schmidt-Rhen, Karl Schuch, Mme. Sinclair, Maria Riezler White, Joseph Wechsberg, Georges Wildenstein, and *Gazette des Beaux-Arts, Kölner Stadt-Anzeiger, The New York Times,* reference books and anonymous sources.

Seurat's "Les Poseuses" (small version), 1888-1975

Seurat's "Les Poseuses" (small version), 1888-1975

1975. 14 panels, 20″ × 30″ (50.8 × 76.2 cm), and one color reproduction of "Les Poseuses", size of original plus frame 23⅜″ × 27¼″ (59.3 × 69.2 cm); all in thin black frames, under glass. Color reproduction: Dia Blauel, Munich.

First exhibited in one-man show at John Weber Gallery, New York, May 1975.

Edition of 3. All owned by H.H.

96

"Les Poseuses"
(small version)
painted 1888, Paris, by

Georges Pierre Seurat

Born 1859, in Paris, 60 rue de Bondy, near the Porte Saint Martin.

His father, Chrysotome-Antoine Seurat, son of a farmer of the Champagne region, belongs to rich Parisian middle class. Retired at age 41 as a minor court official (huissier) of the Tribunal of the Département Seine, at La Villette, then an independent commune north of Paris. Maintains house in le Raincy, near Paris. His mother, Ernestine Faivre, 13 years younger than her husband, is the daughter of a Parisian jeweller. Paul Haumonté-Faivre, his uncle, owns "Au Père de Fouille," prosperous fancy goods store at 48, avenue des Ternes. His brother Émile, a playwright of comedies, with minor success. His sister Marie-Berthe marries Léon Appert, an engineer and glass-maker.

Soon after his birth, family moves to large apartment in newly built neighborhood of 10th arrondissement at 110, boulevard Magenta. 1871, during Paris Commune, escape to Fontainebleau. Attends Lycée until 1876. At age 15, starts taking drawing classes at vocational École Municipale de Dessin with Justin Lequien, an academic sculptor.

1877 student at the École des Beaux-Arts, under Henri Lehmann, a pupil of Ingres. 1879-80 one year of military service in an infantry regiment at Brest, a port in Brittany. Shortens normal 3-5 year service by paying 1,500 francs. Family supports him financially. Does not live from sales of his work. On return to Paris, 1880, takes small studio at 19, rue de Chabrol in Montmartre; later moves to newly constructed building, 128 bis, Boulevard de Clichy.

1883 exhibition of a drawing in the official Salon. 1884 the Salon's jury refuses his first major painting, "La Baignade à Asnières." Together with other rejected artists, he exhibits in the "Salon des Artistes Indépendents," a newly founded artists' collective with exhibition space in the Pavillon de la Ville de Paris on the Champs Elysées. He is a member of its executive committee and exhibits regularly with the group until his death. His friends and followers, Signac, Dubois-Pillet, Angrand, and Luce also belong to the Société des Artistes Indépendents. Camille Pissarro successfully lobbies for his invitation to the 8th impressionist exhibition 1886, against vigorous opposition of Renoir, Monet, Cézanne, and Sisley. Same year, dealer Durand-Ruel exhibits one of his paintings in New York. 1887, 1889 and 1891 exhibitions with Brussels avant-garde group "Les XX."

Draws and paints everyday life scenes, work, leisure, and entertainment of the lower and middle class, landscapes, and seascapes. Frequent painting excursions to industrial suburban Paris and the Atlantic coast. Based on the scientific theories for the optical mixtures of colors and simultaneous contrasts by Blanc, Sutter, Chevreul, Maxwell, Rood, Helmholtz and the writings on the associative expressiveness of lines by Charles Henry, he tries to methodically construct harmony in geometricized compositions according to scientific laws.

These so-called "neo-impressionist," "pointillist," or "divisionist" paintings, composed of myriads of small dots of pure pigment, meet hostility and derision. Few are sold, at low prices. Many are given to his friends as presents. His work is defended and admired by the critic Félix Fénéon and his circle of symbolist writers and poets, including Gustave Kahn, Émile Verhaeren, Paul Adam, Jean Ajalbert, Paul Alexis, and his biographer, Jules Christophe. He shares their sympathies with anarchist communism.

1890 birth of his son, Pierre Georges, from his mistress, Madeleine Knobloch, a 20 year old model. Acknowledges his paternity. Moves with mother and child to 39, passage de l'Elysée-des-Beaux-Arts, now rue André-Antoine, in Montmartre.

Dies, at age 32, probably of meningitis, 1891. His son dies 2 weeks later.

"Les Poseuses"
(small version)
acquired, probably as a present, by

Jules F. Christophe

Born 1840 in Paris. Son of a merchant.

Writer and government official. 1889 appointed Deputy Chief of Staff in the French Ministry of War.

Author of theater plays and fiction. 1887 co-author with Anatole Cerfberr of "Repertoire de la Comédie humaine," a biographical dictionary for Balzac readers. Contributor of theater and art criticism, essays and biographical articles to numerous literary magazines associated with symbolism and anarchist communism. Publishes 1890 one of the early extensive articles on Seurat and his theories ever written, in "Les Hommes d'Aujourd'hui," a symbolist weekly. In the same magazine appear his articles on the painters Dubois-Pillet and Maximilian Luce. He himself is the subject of a biographical sketch by Félix Fénéon in "Les Hommes d'Aujourd'hui."

Closely related to circle of symbolist/anarchist writers and neo-impressionist painters, including Fénéon, Gustave Kahn, Charles Henry, Paul Adam, Jean Ajalbert, Jules Laforgue, Seurat, Signac, Pissarro.

Has strong sympathies with anarchist communism. Contributes to fund for the destitute children of imprisoned anarchists.

Author of Seurat's obituary in "La Plume," 1891.

Reportedly gives his son "Les Poseuses" during his own life time. Date of death unknown.

Detail of Drawing by Dubois-Pillet, 1888

"Les Poseuses"
(small version)
acquired after 1892 by

B.A. Edynski and Max Hochschiller

"Les Poseuses"
(small version)
purchased 1909 by

Josse and Gaston Bernheim-Jeune

Twin brothers born 1870 in Brussels. Father, Alexandre Bernheim, paint manufacturer and merchant in art supplies from Besançon. 1854 moves to Paris to continue business there at 8, rue Lafitte, near the Rothschild family mansion; expands to dealing with contemporary art, helped by the protection of Princess Mathilde and the Duc d'Aumale, son of King Louis Philippe.

Brothers attend Lycée Condorcet, Paris; join their father's business. Their cousins, Jos Hessel and Georges Bernheim, also art dealers. Their sister, Gabrielle, married to painter Félix Valloton.

Move to larger gallery quarters at 25, boulevard de la Madeleine and 15, rue Richepance. Participate in organization of Centennial Exhibition 1900 in Paris and many exhibitions abroad. Assist in building private collections, among them those of the wealthy importer Sergei I. Shchukin and of Morosoff in Moscow; form the collection of the Museum of Tananarive, Madagascar. Charged with sale of important collections. Accredited experts with Appellate Court in Paris. Officers of Legion of Honor.

Artists exhibited and represented are predominantly impressionist, neo-impressionist, and fauvist. Félix Fénéon artistic director for 25 years. Numerous publications by gallery.

1925 gala opening of large new gallery quarters by Gaston Doumergue, the President of France, on corner rue du Faubourg-Saint-Honoré and avenue Matignon, in the immediate neighborhood of the palaces of the French President and Prime Minister.

The family mansion at 107, avenue Henri Martin, has grand salon with 25 foot ceiling, decorated by 80 Renoirs; the walls of the dining room are covered by 30 Cézannes, 20 Toulouse-Lautrecs, an El Greco, and a large Corot. Family also owns a château in the provinces, and maintains several large automobiles and a dirigible balloon.

Gaston has apartment avenue du Maréchal Maunoury, decorated by Raoul Dufy. He, himself, paints landscapes, still lifes, and nudes, under the name Gaston de Villers. His paintings exhibited at the Société Nationale des Beaux-Arts, the Salon d'Automne, and Société des Artistes français. He is co-founder and treasurer and exhibits with the Société coloniale des Artistes français. 1927 retrospective exhibition at Galerie Bernheim-Jeune. Works in French provincial museums.

Brothers actively participate in defense of Alfred Dreyfus, the French officer falsely condemned for treason in an anti-semitic conspiracy. During World War I, gallery's paintings are evacuated to Bordeaux, where French Government also takes refuge. 1940 move to Lyons. Josse Bernheim dies there in 1941. Gaston Bernheim flees German invasion of Lyons. Eventually lives in Monte Carlo. Dies 1953.

Reopening of gallery in Paris 1947.

Painting by Édouard Vuillard, "Gaston and Josse Bernheim," 1912

"Les Poseuses"
(small version)
purchased 1910 for 4,000 ffrs. by

Alphonse Kann

Descendant of family of financial advisors to the courts and aristocracy of Europe. His father, Louis Kann, married to a cousin of Lord Burnham. Her family associated with the English business world. His uncles, Rudolphe and Maurice Kann, build famous art collections in Paris, on the income from gold mines in Transvaal, South Africa. (Rembrandt's "Aristotle Contemplating the Bust of Homer," in Rudolphe Kann collection, now at Metropolitan Museum, New York. Art dealers Gimpel and the brothers Duveen buy the collection 1907, for 17-million ffrs.).

Grows up in Paris. Spends time in London working in business of his mother's family there.

Becomes closely associated with literary and art circles in Paris. Frequently sees Roussel, Cocteau, Éluard, Breton, Picasso, Braque, and is part of Gertrude Stein's "salon."

Owns large eclectic collection, ranging from Egyptian sculpture through archaic, Greek, Roman, Persian, and Chinese art, Pre-Columbian, African and Pacific objects, Romanesque and Gothic sculpture, enamels, ivories, illuminated manuscripts, Coptic works, paintings by Cimabue, Pollaiolo, Tintoretto, Brueghel the Elder, Fabrizius, Rubens, Fragonard, Turner, to period furniture, impressionist works and modern art of the École de Paris.

Often buys and sells on his own, acting as amateur dealer. Recognized by many as arbiter of taste. Advises the banker David-Weill, Arturo Lopez, Charles de Noailles. Assists contemporary art dealer Paul Guillaume.

1920 major auction of part of his collection at Galerie Petit, Paris. 1927 large sale of works at American Art Association in New York, for a total of $282.222.

Inhabits 17th century mansion in St. Germain-en-Laye, near Paris. A convent he owns on Capri is sold to his friend, Princess Margherita of Savoy. Buys castle at Cintra, Portugal.

Escapes to England from German invasion of France. Dies there around 1950.

"Les Poseuses"
(small version)
purchased 1913 or after by

Marius de Zayas

Born 1880 at Vera Cruz, Mexico. Descendant of well-to-do family of Spanish nobility. Father Professor of law and history, judge, publisher of major daily newspaper in Vera Cruz, poet laureate of Mexico and painter; personal friend of Mexican President Porfirio Diaz until his articles, critical of Diaz's increasingly dictatorial regime, lead to break and force family to emigrate to the U.S.

No formal education. Contributes illustrations to *El Diario*, Mexico City newspaper. 1905 first visit to U.S. Settles in New York 1907. Caricaturist for the *New York World*, a daily newspaper.

Joins the circle of Alfred Stieglitz, photographer and promoter of new art. Exhibits 1909 caricatures of New York society figures, theatre, and art personalities, at his Photo-Secession Gallery. Contributes numerous articles on avant-garde art, photography and African art to *Camera Work*, a Stieglitz publication. Frequent visits to Paris 1910-14; meets many avant-garde figures there. With photographer Edward Steichen scouting for new art to be shown at "291" Fifth Avenue, the new Stieglitz gallery. Selects Picasso exhibition there 1911, Braque paintings for 1914 show. 1913 exhibition of his own cubist influenced "abstract" caricatures. Exhibition of African sculpture mainly from his own collection, in 1914-15.

Co-author 1913, of "A Study of the Modern Evolution of Plastic Expression," with his friend Paul B. Haviland, the American representative of Haviland & Co., china manufacturers of Limoges, France. Under Stieglitz's auspices, 1915-16, co-editor with Haviland of the proto-dadaist magazine "291," with contributions from Picabia, Man Ray, Duchamp, and others.

1915 establishment of Modern Gallery at 500 Fifth Avenue. His partners are Picabia, Haviland and Agnes Ernst Meyer, wife of Eugene Meyer, a financier and high government official. He collaborates with her on dadaist poems.

1918 establishment of his own gallery at 549 Fifth Avenue. Deals in modern European, African and Mexican art and builds sizable collection. Closes in early 1920's. Continues as private dealer, collaborates on exhibitions and serves as agent for Paris dealers Durand-Ruel, Paul Rosenberg, and Paul Guillaume.

First marriage ends in divorce, 2 daughters. Second marriage 1925 to Virginia Randolph Harrison, a woman 21 years his junior. Her father, a lawyer, ex-Congressman (D.) and U.S. Governor General of Philippine Islands (1913-21). Her mother Mary Crocker, daughter of Charles Crocker, the builder of the Central Pacific Railroad.

Move to Austrian mountain resort St. Anton. Gives up art dealing. 1928 purchase of 14th century château at Monestier de Clermont near Grenoble, France. Derives income from sales of his collection and his wife's fortune.

In the early thirties filmmaking in Spain, documentaries on flamenco music and bullfight. During war years with wife, daughter (born 1927) and son Rodrigo (born 1939) at French château pursuing studies in cryptology and musicology.

1947 move to U.S. Buys house in Greenwich, Conn. Resumes documentary filmmaking.

Dies 1961 of coronary thrombosis in Hartford, Conn.

Photo by Alfred Stieglitz

"Les Poseuses"
(small version)
purchased 1922 for $5,500 by

John Quinn

Born 1870 Tiffin, Ohio. Son of Irish immigrants. Father James William Quinn, prosperous baker in Fostoria, Ohio. Mother Mary Quinlan, orphan. Sister Julia married to William V. Anderson, successful pharmacist of Fostoria. Sister Clara nun of Ursuline Convent, Tiffin.

Graduate of Fostoria High School. 1888 at University of Michigan. 1890-93 in Washington, D.C., as private secretary of Secretary of the Treasury Charles Foster (friend of Quinn family), under President Benjamin Harrison. Graduates from Georgetown University Law School 1893, Harvard University Law School 1895.

1893 clerkship in New York law firm of General Benjamin F. Tracy. 1900 junior partner with Alexander & Colby. 1906 own law practice specializing in financial and corporate law. Offices at 31 Nassau Street in Wall Street district.

Chief Counsel to National Bank of Commerce, second largest bank in U.S. Instrumental in acquisition of Equitable Life Assurance Society by Thomas Ryan, financier with extensive interests in coal, tobacco, Congolese and Angolan diamond mining. His chief counsel as of 1906. Negotiates merger of Bowling Green Trust and Madison Trust with Equitable Trust, 1908-1909. New York Stock Exchange counsel on tax law, 1913. Special counsel to N.Y. State Comptroller in inheritance tax proceedings against estate of John Jacob Astor, 1914. Represents munitions makers in Federal Tax case, 1917. Submits brief in Congress for adoption of Alien Property Act, same year. Represents U.S. Alien Property Custodian and private American interests in suit over seizure of German properties. Wins 1920 in U.S. Supreme Court establishing the law's constitutionality (legal fee $174,000).

Tammany Hall Democrat. Delegate to National Convention 1908 and 1912. Campaigns for candicacy of Oscar W. Underwood against Woodrow Wilson. Theodore Roosevelt a personal friend.

Staunch supporter of Irish causes. Contemptuous of American cultural life, francophile, anti-semitic, anti-German; proposes to French President Poincare take-over of German Ruhr industries by Allies, 1923.

Collects 19th and 20th century French and English painting and sculpture, including Cézanne, van Gogh, Gauguin, Seurat, Derain, Matisse, Picasso, Duchamp-Villon, Brancusi, Epstein. Investment in art estimated at $500,000. Has personal contact with artists in Paris and London. Helps with organization and promotion of Armory Show, 1913. Conducts successful campaign in Congress for the exemption of modern art from customs duty. Wins in Congress tax exemption of art sales by living artists, 1918.

Sponsors U.S. tours of Irish writers and theater productions. Assists in the publication of works by W. B. Yeats, J. M. Synge, Joseph Conrad, T. S. Eliot, James Joyce. Extensive correspondence with writers. Buys literary manuscripts, including all of Joseph Conrad's. Sells most in auction 1923 (Conrad for $110,000 and Joyce's "Ulysses" for $2,000). Defends "Ulysses" against obscenity charges in New York Court.

Lives, as of 1911, in top floor apartment at 58 Central Park West. Frequent travels to Ireland, England, and France. Remains bachelor, though has several romances.

Member of numerous exclusive clubs, of Contemporary Art Society, and Société de Cent Bibliophiles. 1915 appointed Honorary Fellow of Metropolitan Museum, 1918 Chevalier of Legion of Honor.

Dies of cancer in New York, 1924.

Photo around 1921. From "The Man from New York," by B. L. Reid

"Les Poseuses"
(small version)
inherited 1924 by

Julia Quinn Anderson

Born 1880 in Fostoria, Ohio. Daughter of Irish immigrants. Her father William Quinn, prosperous baker in Fostoria. Her mother, Mary Quinlan, orphan. Her sister, Clara, nun at Ursuline Convent, Tiffin, Ohio. Her brother, John Quinn, well-known New York lawyer and collector of books and modern art.

Marries William Vincent Anderson 1903, a prosperous pharmacist of Fostoria. 1907 birth of daughter Mary, only child.

Beginning 1914 frequent and extended visits to New York, often acting as hostess for her bachelor brother, John Quinn. Daughter attends school in the city. Around 1919 permanent move of the family to New York, after sale of Fostoria business.

Major beneficiary of John Quinn's estate on his death 1924.

Dies of cancer 1934.

Photo courtesy Dr. James F. Conroy

"Les Poseuses"
(small version)
inherited 1934 by

Mary Anderson Conroy

Born in Cleveland, Ohio, 1907. Her father, William Vincent Anderson, prosperous pharmacist in Fostoria, Ohio. Her mother, Julia Quinn, daughter of a prosperous baker in Fostoria, sister of John Quinn, a well-known New York Lawyer and collector of books and modern art.

Frequent visits to John Quinn in New York. Family eventually settles in the City, at 37 West 93 Street, after sale of business in Fostoria.

Attends school at the Convent of the Sacred Heart in New York 1914, and Maplehurst High School in Upper Manhattan.

Extensive travels abroad with her mother or friends. Engaged in volunteer charity work. Unpaid assistant of Mrs. Cornelius Sullivan, a co-founder of the Museum of Modern Art and a private art dealer.

At her mother's death, 1934, principal beneficiary of inheritance, including numerous works from the collection of the late John Quinn.

1941 marriage to Thomas F. Conroy, M.D., a urological surgeon of New York. Volunteer paramedical work. After World War II move to San Mateo, California. 1946 birth of only child, Thomas Anthony Conroy.

Dies of cancer, 1970.

Photo around 1950, courtesy Dr. Thomas F. Conroy

"Les Poseuses"
(small version)
purchased 1936 through Mrs. Cornelius Sullivan for $40,000 by

Henry P. McIlhenny

Born 1910 Philadelphia, Pennsylvania. Descendant of wealthy Irish family of Philadelphia society.

His father John D. McIlhenny, member of boards of directors of several large gas companies; partner of Helme & McIlhenny, manufacturers of gas meters in Philadelphia; member of the board of managers of Savings Fund Society of Germantown, Pa. Collector of European decorative arts, oriental rugs and paintings. President of Pennsylvania Museum and School of Industrial Art (now Philadelphia Museum of Art) and Director of Philadelphia Art Alliance.

His mother Frances Galbraith Plumer. Collector of 19th and early 20th century art. Trustee of Philadelphia Museum.

His uncle Francis S. McIlhenny, lawyer; vice president of Sun Oil Company; member of Board of Directors of numerous large corporations; member of Pennsylvania Senate (1907-15); director and officer of YMCA.

His sister Mrs. John (Bernice) Wintersteen married to lawyer. Collector of 19th and early 20th century art. Trustee and President (1964-68) of Philadelphia Museum of Art.

Studied at Episcopal Academy and Milton Academy, elite prep schools near Philadelphia and Boston. Bachelor of Arts 1933, Harvard; graduate studies in art history, 1933-34, Harvard, under Prof. Paul J. Sachs.

Curator of Decorative Arts at Philadelphia Museum of Art 1935-64. Since 1964 trustee and 1968 vice president of the Museum. Member Smithsonian Art Commission, Washington. 1949-62 director of Philadelphia Orchestra Association and Metropolitan Opera Association, New York.

Served to Lieutenant Commander in U.S. Naval Reserve. During World War II on active duty.

Major part of his collection purchased with his mother's financial backing during depression: silver, period furniture, and predominantly 19th century French painting and sculpture, including Cézanne, Chardin, Daumier, David, Degas, Delacroix, van Gogh, Ingres, Matisse, Renoir, Rouault, Toulouse-Lautrec, Vuillard.

Bachelor, frequent society host in his mansion, 2 adjoining mid-19th century town houses, with ballroom, on Rittenhouse Square in Philadelphia. Employs 8 servants there. Spends part of year at Victorian Glenveagh Castle, his property in County Donegal, Ireland; maintained by 30 servants.

Member of Philadelphia Club and Rittenhouse Club, in Philadelphia, Century Association and Grolier Club in New York.

Together with Seurat's "Les Poseuses" buys Picasso's "L'Arlequin" from Mrs. Mary Anderson Conroy, for a total of $52,500. Her friend, Mrs. Cornelius Sullivan, co-founder of the Museum of Modern Art, New York, and a private art dealer, receives a commission of 10%.

Photo by Richard Noble, New York

"Les Poseuses"
(small version)
$1,033,200 auction bid at Christie's, 1970, half share held by

Artemis S.A.

Incorporated April 2, 1970 in the Grand Duchy of Luxembourg; private holding company of subsidiaries incorporated in the United Kingdom (David Carritt, Ltd., London) and other countries. Invests and trades in works of the fine and decorative arts of all periods and cultures.

Inventory included old masters, impressionists, classical modern art, contemporary art; antique, African, Asian sculpture; decorative silver.

Collaborating art dealers include E.V. Thaw & Co., New York; Fourcade, Droll, Inc., New York; R.M. Light & Co., Boston; Heinz Berggruen & Cie., Paris; Heinz Herzer & Co., Munich; P. & D. Colnaghi, London; Heim, London; Lefevre, London; Fischer Fine Art, London.

Works sold among others to National Gallery, Washington; Cleveland Museum; Norton Simon Foundation; Ashmolean Museum, Oxford.

Board of Directors

Baron Léon Lambert. Chairman since 1970. Chairman of Compagnie Bruxelles Lambert.

Eugene Victor Thaw, managing director since 1974. Head of E.V. Thaw & Co. Private dealer. 1970-72 President of Art Dealers Association of America, Inc.

David Carritt, since 1970. Head of David Carritt Ltd., Artemis subsidiary in London. Old Master expert, formerly with Christie's, London.

Count Christian zu Salm-Reifferscheidt, 1970-73. Art historian, expert in antique art. Former curator of Bavarian State Museum, Munich. Deceased.

Philippe R. Stoclet, since 1970. Former representative of Loeb, Rhoades & Co., New York. Chief executive officer of Brussels financing company. Descendant of Alphonse Stoclet, international railroad builder and collector, who commissioned architect Josef Hoffmann of "Wiener Werkstätten" to build Palais Stoclet, Brussels.

Count Artur Strachwitz, since 1970. Born 1905. Brother-in-law of Prince of Liechtenstein. Former cultural attaché at Brussels Embassy of German Federal Republic.

Baron Alexis de Rédé, since 1970. Financial consultant, collector. Among major beneficiaries of inheritance of his late friend, Arturo Lopez, South American financier. Lives in 17th century Hôtel Lambert, Paris, rue St. Louis en Ile, now owned by Baron Guy de Rothschild, a friend.

Walter Bareiss, since 1973. Born Tübingen, Germany. Chairman of family business Schachenmeyr, Mann & Cie. GmbH., Salach, Germany, yarn factory. Chairman of Cobar Industries, Inc. Served in U.S. Army in World War II. Married to Molly Stimson, cousin of Henry L. Stimson, late US Secretary of War. Collector. Member collection committee 20th century art, chairman Gallery Association Bavarian State Museum, Munich. Trustee Museum of Modern Art, New York, 1964-73, acting director 1969-70, member committee on drawings and prints. Lives Munich and Greenwich, Conn.

Heinz Berggruen, since 1974. Head of Paris art gallery, Heinz Berggruen & Cie..

Art Advisory Board

Baron and Baroness Élie de Rothschild, 1970-73; Prof. Abraham Hammacher, 1970-73; Douglas Cooper, 1971-73; Roderic Thesiger, 1971-73; Heinz Herzer, since 1971; Count Cesare Cicogna Mozzoni, 1972-73; Valentine Abdy, since 1974.

Holding Company and Subsidiaries

Year	consolidated profit	total assets	assets works of art at cost
1970-71	$ 43,042	$ 5,431,299	$2,207,680
1971-72	641,992	5,703,195	3,676,507
1972-73	778,448	8,010,350	5,787,507
1973-74	733,397	10,256,991	7,864,400

Authorized capital: 1,000,000 shares of $10 nominal value per share. Issued capital: 413,025 shares of $10 each: $4,130,250 (Oct. 1974).

"Les Poseuses"
(small version)
half share held by Artemis S.A. under chairmanship of

Baron Léon Lambert

Born Etterbeek—Brussels, 1928.

His grandfather, Léon Lambert, official agent of Paris Rothschild Bank in Belgium. Banker of King Léopold II, who gives him title of Baron, in recognition of his services as financier of Belgian colonization of Central Africa. Married to Lucie de Rothschild-Anspach, daughter of Baron Gustave de Rothschild. Their daughter marries Rudolf de Goldschmidt-Rothschild of Naples.

His father, Baron Henri Lambert, head of Banque Lambert, Brussels; correspondent of Rothschild banks in Paris and London, with extensive interests in the Belgian Congo, radio, and airline. His mother, Baroness Hansi von Reininghaus, of Austrian nobility. After her husband's death, 1933, titular head of bank while leaving affairs in hands of trusted bankers (bank survives German occupation of Belgium in WW II intact). Collector; sponsor of cultural events. Dies 1960.

During World War II, with his mother, brother Philippe, and sister, in England and the U.S. Studies at Yale, Oxford, Geneva. Licencié ès science politique, University of Geneva.

1949 assumes role in Banque Lambert, S.C.S., Brussels, a limited partnership. 1950 senior partner and chairman. 1953 absorption of Banque de reports et de dépôts. Rapid expansion of financial interests 1966 vice-Chairman, 1971 chairman of holding Compagnie Lambert pour l'industrie et la finance; through merger with De Launoit family's interests 1972, holding becomes Belgium's second largest. Under the new name Compagnie Bruxelles Lambert, extensive international interests in banks, insurance companies, real estate, retailing, public utilities, oil, steel, and metallurgy. 1974 merger with Banque Bruxelles makes Banque Bruxelles Lambert Belgium's second largest commercial bank. Retains extensive business and family ties with Rothschild banking group.

Chairman of: Banque Lambert, S.C.S., Brussels; Compagnie Bruxelles Lambert pour la finance et l'industrie, Brussels; SOGES, Brussels; Compagnie de constructions civiles, Brussels; La Concorde S.A., Brussels; The Lambert Brussels Corporation, New York; Artemis S.A., Luxembourg; Manufacture Belge de Lampes et de Matériel Électronique (M.B.L.E.), Brussels.

Vice Chairman of: Select Risk Investments S.S., Luxembourg; Electrobel S.A., Brussels; Lambert Milanese S.p.A.

Member of Board of Directors of: Magnum Fund Ltd., Toronto; Petrofina S.A., Brussels; Berliner Handelsgesellschaft, Frankfurt-Main; Five Arrows Securities Co. Ltd., Toronto; Banca d'America e d'Italia, Milan; New Court Securities Corporation, New York; INNO-B.M.S.A., Brussels; ELECTROGAZ S.A., Brussels; ITALUNION, Luxembourg; General Fund International Management Co., Luxembourg; General Fund International S.A., Luxembourg; General Fund International Holding Co., Luxembourg; United Overseas Bank. Geneva; Compagnie Auxilière Internationale des Chemins de Fer.

Member Advisory Board of: Société Financière pour les Pays d'Outre-Mer (SFOM), Geneva.

1964 move into new bank building at 24, avenue Marnix, designed by Gordon Bunshaft of architecture firm Skidmore, Owings & Merrill, New York. Large Henry Moore sculpture on street level plaza.

Bachelor. Lives in penthouse apartment above bank. Apartment and banking floors house large collection of classical modern art, partially inherited from his mother, non-western and contemporary European and American art. Board member of Société Philharmonique de Bruxelles, Musée du Cinéma, Cinémathèque Royale de Belgique, Jeune Peintre Belge.

Decorations: Chevalier de l'Ordre de Léopold (Belgium), Commandeur de l'Ordre à la Valeur (Cameroon), Grande Ufficiale al Merito della Repubblica Italiana (Italy).

According to his wishes, Seurat's "Les Poseuses" exhibited at Bavarian State Museum, Munich.

Photo from "Banque Lambert," Brussels, 1964

"Les Poseuses"
(small version)
bid at Christie's auction and half share held by

Richard L. Feigen

Born 1930, Chicago, Ill. His father, Arthur P. Feigen, a lawyer. His mother Shirley Bierman.

Graduates with B.A. from Yale University 1952, M.B.A. of Harvard Business School, 1954. Begins to collect art.

1955-56 work in business of a relative. Becomes treasurer and member of Investment Committee of Beneficial Standard Life Insurance Company, Los Angeles, and Fidelity Interstate Life Insurance Company, Philadelphia. Member of Board of Directors and Finance Committee, Union Casualty and Life Insurance Company, Mount Vernon, New York.

1956 buys seat on New York Stock Exchange. Sells it 1957.

1957 opens art gallery in Chicago, Richard L. Feigen & Co., Inc., of which he is President and Director. Frequently exhibits contemporary artists. 1963 opening of New York gallery, dealing with old masters and exhibiting contemporary art. Stages "Richard J. Daley" show, 1968, at Chicago gallery, in protest against Chicago police conduct in confrontations with demonstrators during Democratic Convention. Chicago gallery closes 1972. Gives up showroom in New York, 1973; continues as private dealer of predominantly old masters and classical modern art. Since 1965 member and 1974, on Board of Directors of Art Dealers Association of America.

1966 Faculty member, University for Presidents, Young Presidents Organization, Phoenix, Arizona. Lectures on "Art for Your Business" and "Art for the Private Collector." Founder of Art for Business, Inc., now an inactive corporate shell.

1963 Member of the Advisory Board of Independent Voters of Illinois. 1964 on Honorary Steering Committee, Young Citizens for Johnson. 1972 unsuccessful bid to be elected alternate delegate to Democratic Convention supporting McGovern's Presidential candidacy. Member American Civil Liberties Union.

1966 marriage to Sandra Elizabeth Canning Walker. Has two children and three step-children.

In his auction bid for Seurat's "Les Poseuses," represents his own interests and the interests of ARTEMIS S.A., a Luxembourg-based art investment holding company. Armand Hammer, Chairman of Occidental Petroleum Corp., puts in one bid, then gives up.

110

"Les Poseuses"
(small version)
purchased 1971 for unknown amount (part in art works) by

Heinz Berggruen

Born 1914 in Berlin, Germany.

Studies art history in Berlin and Toulouse, France, graduating there with equivalent of Master of Fine Art degree. In late 1930's moves to California. Postgraduate studies in art history at Berkeley. Assistant Curator of San Francisco Museum of Art. Writes art criticism for *San Francisco Chronicle*. Works at 1939 World Exposition on Treasure Island, San Francisco.

Marries Lilian Zellerbach of prominent San Francisco paper manufacturing family. Birth of son John Berggruen 1943 (now art dealer in San Francisco). Birth of daughter Helen, 1945.

After World War II, service in US Army. Stationed in England and Germany. Works for German language US Army publication in Munich.

Around 1947 move to Paris via Zurich. Employed by cultural division of UNESCO. In late 1940's, starts dealing in art books and prints. Becomes art dealer. Berggruen & Cie, now at 70, rue de l'Université, develops into one of major Parisian art dealers in modern art, particularly Ecole de Paris.

Lives Ile St. Louis, Paris, and on château near Pontoise. Owns large collection.

1974 elected member of the Board of Directors of Artemis S.A., a Luxembourg-based art investment holding company. Chevalier of Legion of Honor.

His purchase of Seurat's *Les Poseuses* at "impressive profit" to Artemis S.A. (annual report). Painting now on anonymous loan in Bavarian State Museum, Munich.

Photo from "Art in America," 1963

The gathering of information for this work was assisted by the publications of, or personal communication with:

American Art Association, Art Dealers Association of America, Inc., Artemis S.A., Banque Lambert, Alfred Barr Jr., John Berggruen, Galerie Bernheim-Jeune, Leslie Bernstein, Hélène Bokanovski, Jules Christophe, Jean Clay, Leslie Cohen, James F. Conroy, Lucie Cousturier, Henri Dauberville, Henri Dorra, Albert Dubois-Pillet, Donald Drew Egbert, Richard L. Feigen, Félix Fénéon, Isi Fiszman, Andreas Freund, Edward Fry, Jean-Claude Garot, Réné Gimpel, Grace Glueck, Louis Gordon, Jonathan Green, Gilbert Gruet, Joan Ungersma Halperin, César M. de Hauke, Eugenia Herbert, Robert L. Herbert, Maurice Jardot, Claude Roger Marx, Henry P. McIlhenny, Gilles Neret, Robert Noble, Dorothy Norman, Patrick O'Higgins, Henri Perruchot, Alan Pryce-Jones, B. L. Reid, Jean Renoir, George Henri Rivière, John Rewald, Alexandre Rosenberg, John Russell, Volker Schierk, Germain Seligman, Gertrude Stein, Alfred Stieglitz, Jean Sutter, Gerda Winzer-Hoog, Leopold Zahn, Rodrigo de Zayas, and *Art in America, Business Management, Business Week, France Soir, The New York Times, L'Oeil, The Philadelphia Inquirer, Le Soir, The Times, Time,* reference books and anonymous sources.

On Social Grease

On Social Grease*

1975. 6 placques, 30″ × 30″ (76.2 × 76.2 cm), photoengraved magnesium plates mounted on aluminum with dull finish. Photographs: Walter Russell, New York.

First exhibited in one-man show at John Weber Gallery, New York.

Coll. Gilman Paper Co., New York.

Family business, founded 1881 by Isaac Gilman in Gilman, Vermont. Now headed in third generation by Howard Gilman, chairman of the board, and Charles Gilman Jr., president. Paper and pulp industry, St. Mary's Georgia, with over 225,000 acres of company owned timberland and own railroad. Headquarters: Time-Life building, New York.

*Title inspired through remark by Carl Andre.

Perhaps the most important single reason for the increased interest of international corporations in the arts is the almost limitless diversity of projects which are possible.

These projects can be tailored to a company's specific business goals and can return dividends far out of proportion to the actual investment required.

C. Douglas Dillon

C. Douglas Dillon

Metropolitan Museum, President
Business Committee for the Arts, Co-founder, first Chairman
Rockefeller Foundation, Chairman
Brookings Institution, Chairman

U.S. & Foreign Securities Corp., Chairman
Dillon, Read & Co., Chairman of Exec. Com., Director

Quoted from C. Douglas Dillion "Cross-Cultural Communication Through the Arts",
in *Columbia Journal of World Business,* Columbia University, New York, Sept./Oct. 1971.

My appreciation and enjoyment of art are esthetic rather than intellectual.

I am not really concerned with what the artist means; it is not an intellectual operation—it is what I feel.

Nelson Rockefeller

Nelson Rockefeller

Museum of Modern Art, Trustee
Vice President of the United States of America

Quoted from report by Grace Glueck, *The New York Times,* May 1, 1969, page 50.

But the significant thing is that increasing recognition in the business world that the arts are not a thing apart,

that they have to do with all aspects of life, including business—

that they are, in fact, essential to business.

Frank Stanton

Frank Stanton

American Crafts Council, Trustee
Business Committee for the Arts, Chairman
Carnegie Institution, Washington D.C., Trustee
Lincoln Center for the Performing Arts, Director
Rockefeller Foundation, Trustee
Atlantic Richfield Co., Director
American Electric Power Co., Inc., Director, Member
    Exec. Com.

CBS Inc., Vice Chairman, Director
Diebold Venture Capital Corp., Director
New Perspective Fund, Director
New York Life Insurance Co., Director, Member Exec. Com.
Pan American World Airways, Inc., Director, Member
    Exec. Com.
Rand Corporation, Trustee
Roper Public Opinion Research Center, Director

Quoted from Frank Stanton "The Arts—A Challenge to Business", speech to 25th Anniversary Public Relations Conference of Public Relations Society of American and Canadian Public Relations Society, Detroit, Nov. 12, 1972.

From an economic standpoint, such involvement in the arts can mean direct and tangible benefits.

It can provide a company with extensive publicity and advertising, a brighter public reputation, and an improved corporate image.

It can build better customer relations, a readier acceptance of company products, and a superior appraisal of their quality.

Promotion of the arts can improve the morale of employees and help attract qualified personnel.

David Rockefeller

David Rockefeller

Museum of Modern Art, Vice Chairman
Business Committee for the Arts, Co-founder and Director

Chase Manhattan Bank Corp., Chairman, Chief Exec. Officer

Quoted from David Rockefeller "Culture and the Corporation's Support of the Arts", speech to National Industrial Conference Board, Sept. 20, 1966.

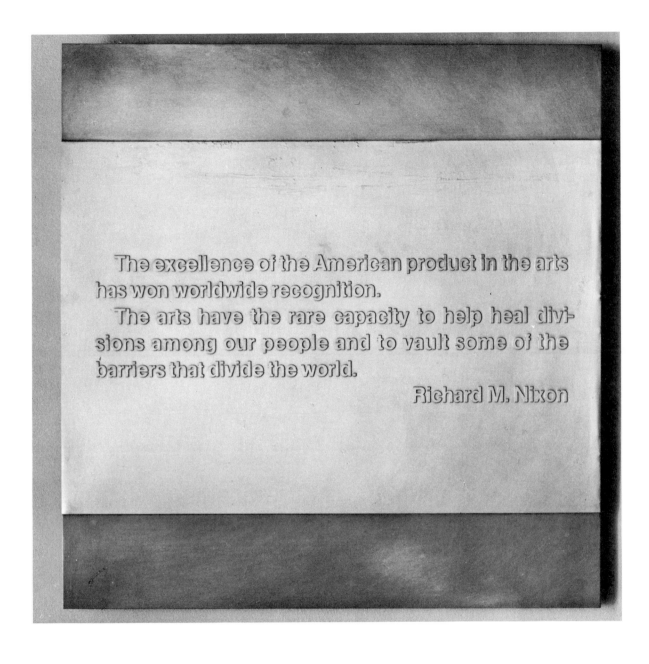

Richard M. Nixon

President of the United States 1968-74 (resigned)

Quoted from address to Congress in support of the National Endowment for the Arts, in *The Wall Street Journal,* Jan. 2, 1970, page 6.

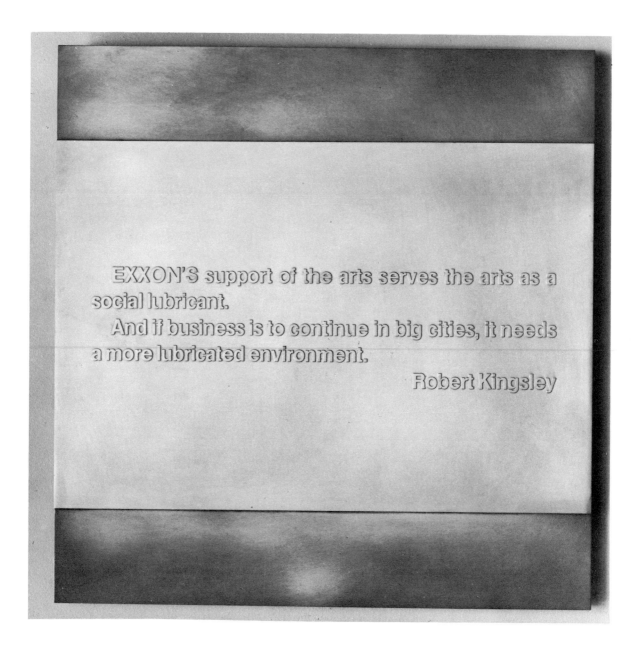

Robert Kingsley

Manager of Urban Affairs in
Department of Public Affairs, Exxon Corp., New York
President, Arts and Business Council, New York

Quoted in Marylin Bender "Business Aids the Arts . . . And Itself",
The New York Times, Oct. 20, 1974, section III, page 1.

Robert Kingsley, posing in front of plaque with quote of his, during one-man show at John Weber Gallery, New York, May 1975.

Photo: Impact Photo, Inc., New York.

Selected bibliography
relating to socio-political works

1969

Sello, Gottfried. "Ein Bett ist ein Bett ist . . .", *Die Zeit,* Hamburg, October 10, 1969

Thwaites, John A. "Vom Baum der Kunsterkenntnis.", *Saarbrücker Zeitung,* Saarbrücken, October 14, 1969

von Bonin, Wibke. "Germany: October 1969", *Arts Magazine,* New York, November 1969

Andrea, Christopher. "Haacke explains his astonishing show", *The Christian Science Monitor,* Boston, November 20, 1969

1970

Kramer, Hilton. "Show at the Modern Raises Questions", *The New York Times,* New York, July 2, 1970

Genauer, Emily. "Some Explanations of Information", *Newsday,* Garden City, Long Island, N.Y., July 11, 1970

Perreault, John. "Information", *The Village Voice,* New York, July 16, 1970

Strelow, Hans. "Das grosse Spiel mit den Medien — 'Information', eine Schau im Museum of Modern Art in New York", *Frankfurter Allgemeine Zeitung,* Frankfurt, August 10, 1970

Vinklers, Bitite. "Art and Information — 'Software' at the Jewish Museum", *Arts Magazine,* New York, Sept./Oct., 1970

Ashton, Dore. "New York Commentary", *Studio International,* London, November 1970, Vol. 180, No. 927

Clay, Jean. "Aspects of Bourgeois Art: The World as it is", *Studio International,* London, December 1970, Vol. 180, No. 928

Baker, Kenneth. "New York — Software", *Artforum,* New York, December 1970

1971

Aue, Walter. *P.C.A. – Projekte, Concepte & Aktionen,* DuMont Schauberg, Cologne, 1971

Taylor, John Lloyd. *Directions 3: Eight Artists,* exhibition-catalogue, Milwaukee Art Center, 1971

Tuchman, Maurice. *A & T — A Report on the Art and Technology Program of the Los Angeles County Museum of Art 1967-1971,* Los Angeles County Museum, 1971

Vitt, Walter. "Die Prozesse hinter dem Sichtbaren — Arbeiten von Hans Haacke in der Kölner Galerie Maenz", *Aachener Nachrichten,* Aachen, January 19, 1971

Ott, Günther. "Kennen Sie Manhattan? — Neue Galerie zeigt 720 Fotos von Hans Haacke", *Kölnische Rundschau,* Cologne, January 23, 1971

Pfeiffer, Günter. "Die Front der Puristen — Das Galerieprogramm in der Kölner Lindenstrasse", *Frankfurter Allgemeine Zeitung,* Frankfurt, February 9, 1971

Pfeiffer, Günter. "Ausstellungen — Hans Haacke", *Das Kunstwerk,* Stuttgart, March 1971

Glueck, Grace. "The Guggenheim Cancels Haacke's Show", *The New York Times,* New York, April 7, 1971

Gratz, Roberta. "The Guggenheim Refuses to Hang Slum-lords", *New York Post,* New York, April 8, 1971

Herzig, Doris. "Art Show Scrubbed as Politically Dirty", *Newsday,* Garden City, Long Island, N.Y., April 9, 1971

Perreault, John. "Art — Political Items", *The Village Voice,* New York, April 15, 1971

CBS Newsradio 88, New York. Series of interviews with Edward Fry, Hans Haacke, Thomas Hoving, Thomas Messer in reference to cancellation of Haacke show at Guggenheim Museum, April 25-May 2, 1971

"Haacke-Ausstellung: Fehler im System". *Der Spiegel,* Hamburg, April 26, 1971

CBS Television, 6 o'clock News. Interview with Edward Fry, Hans Haacke, Thomas Messer, conducted by Leonard Harris, New York, April 27, 1971

McFadden, Robert D. "Guggenheim Aide Ousted in Dispute — Edward Fry set up show by Haacke on Slums", *The New York Times,* New York, April 27, 1971

Genauer, Emily. "Art and Artists", *New York Post,* New York, April 27, 1971

Glueck, Grace. "Ousted Curator Assails Guggenheim", *The New York Times,* New York, May 1, 1971

Les chroniques de l'art vivant. "On décroche (toujours) au Guggenheim", Paris, May 1971

Siegel, Jeanne. "An Interview with Hans Haacke", *Arts Magazine,* New York, May 1971

Akston, Joseph J. "Editorial", *Arts Magazine,* New York, May 1971

Fry, Edward. "Hans Haacke, the Guggenheim: The Issues", *Arts Magazine,* New York, May 1971

Baker, Elizabeth C. "Editorial — Artists vs. Museums", *Art News,* New York, May 1971

Burnham, Jack. "Hans Haacke's Cancelled Show at The Guggenheim", *Artforum,* New York, June 1971

"Haacke interdit". *Robho,* No. 5/6, Paris, 1971

Akston, Joseph J. "Editorial", *Arts Magazine,* New York, June 1971

Messer, Thomas. "Guest Editorial", *Arts Magazine,* New York, June 1971

"Gurgles around the Guggenheim". *Studio International,* London, June 1971

"Haacke's one-man show cancelled". *Asahi Journal,* in *Asahi Shimbun,* Tokyo, June 4, 1971

Battcock, Gregory. "New York — One", *Art and Artists,* London, July 1971

Nakahara, Yusuke. "Haacke's one-man show is cancelled. His work deemed too socialist. Politics and Art: Example the Guggenheim Museum", *Bijutsu Techo,* Tokyo, July 1971

Reise, Barbara. "A tale of two exhibitions: The aborted Haacke and Robert Morris Shows", *Studio International,* London, July/August 1971

Reise, Barbara. "Which is in fact what happened — Thomas Messer in an interview with Barbara Reise, April 25, 1971", *Studio International,* London July/August 1971

Alloway, Lawrence. "Art", *The Nation,* New York, August 2, 1971

"Buren, Haacke, chi altro?". *Data,* Milan, September 1971

Haacke, Hans. Letter to the Editor "Editorial — Artists vs. Museums continued", *Art News,* New York, September 1971

Baker, Elisabeth C. Response to Haacke letter to the editor "Editorial — Artists vs. Museums continued", *Art News,* New York, September 1971

1972

Benthall, Jonathan. *Science and Technology in Art Today,* Thames and Hudson, London, 1972 (also Praeger, New York)

Fry, Edward F. *Hans Haacke — Werkmonographie,* with texts by Hans Haacke, DuMont Schauberg, Serie Kunst-Praxis, Cologne, 1972

Haryu, Ichiro. *Art as Action and Concept*, Kodansha Ltd., Tokyo, 1972

Hunter, Sam. *American Art of the 20th Century*, Harry M. Abrams, New York, 1972

Meyer, Ursula. *Conceptual Art*, E.P. Dutton & Co., Inc., New York, 1972

Thomas, Karin. *Kunst – Praxis heute: Eine Dokumentation der aktuellen Ästhetik*, incl. an interview with Hans Haacke, Du Mont Schauberg, Cologne, 1972

Wember, Paul. *Hans Haacke*, exhibition catalogue, Museum Haus Lange, Krefeld, 1972

Haacke, Hans. "Shapolsky et al Manhattan Immobilienbesitz, ein gesellschaftliches Realzeitsystem, Stand 1.3.1972", *Interfunktionen*, No. 9, Cologne, 1972

Smith, Terry. "Evaluating photographs — Investing in some real estate", *The Review*, Sydney, January 1972

Trini, Tommaso. "Mostre — Hans Haacke", *Domus*, Milan, February 1972

Fry, Edward F. "The Post Liberal Artist", *Art and Artist*, London, February 1972

Gutzmer, Manfred. "Die Kunst und das Abwässer- Problem," *Rheinische Post*, Düsseldorf, May 19, 1972. Reprint in *Kunstjahrbuch 3*, Fackelträger, Hannover, 1973.

Frese, Hans M. "Kunst und Abwasser — Wer geht da schon hin?", *Neue Rhein-Zeitung*, Düsseldorf, May 25, 1972

"Hans Haacke", *Flash Art*, Milan, May/July 1972

Sello, Gottfried. "Kunstkalender", *Die Zeit*, Hamburg, June 30, 1972

"Mickey Mouse befragt die Wirklichkeit". *Der Spiegel*, Hamburg, July 3, 1972

Krüger, Werner. "Bohnen wachsen im Museum", *Kölner Stadtanzeiger*, Cologne, July 7, 1972

"Documenta — jung, arm, links". *Der Spiegel*, Hamburg, August 21, 1972

Dickson, David. "Art Politic", *Art and Artists*, London, September 1972

Riese, Hans Peter. "Schmutzaufwühlend?", *Frankfurter Allgemeine Zeitung*, Frankfurt, September 12, 1972

Loetterle, Fred. "Megalopolis Hits Columbus Circle", *Sunday News*, New York, October 15, 1972

Huxtable, Ada Louise. "Megalopolis Show: Artists and the Urban Scene", *The New York Times*, October 31, 1972

Thwaites, John A. and Haacke, Hans. "Interview", *Art and Artists*, London, November 1972

Thwaites, John A. "Cologne", *Art and Artists*, London, November 1972

Davis, Douglas. "Art of the Real (Estate)", *Newsweek*, New York, November 6, 1972

Kuhn, Annette. "Haacke & the landlords — The art that exposed patterns of property", *The Village Voice*, New York, December 14, 1972

Mayer, Rosemary. "Andre, Haacke, Holt, James, Obering — John Weber Gallery", *Arts Magazine*, New York, December 1972

1973

Czartoryska, Urszula. *"Od Pop-Artu do Sztuki Konceptualnej"*, Warsaw, 1973

Haacke, Hans. In *Selbstdarstellung – Künstler über sich*, Herzogenrath, Wulf (editor), (Transcript of talk by Hans Haacke at Folkwang Museum, Essen, June 1972), Droste, Düsseldorf 1973

Hohmeyer, Jürgen. "Rede, Künstler", in *Kunstjahrbuch 3*, Fackelträger, Hannover 1973

Haacke, Hans. "Profil de l'habitat des visiteurs de la galérie", *art press*, Paris, December/January 1973

Winter, Peter. "Kunst im politischen Kampf", *Kunstforum International*, Mainz, Vol. 1, No. 2/3, 1973

Glozer, Laszlo. "Acht Modelle politischer Kunst", *Süddeutsche Zeitung*, München, April 1973

Perreault, John. "Documenting an art-world inside job", *The Village Voice*, New York, May 10, 1973

Boice, Bruce. "Hans Haacke — John Weber Gallery Visitors' Profile", *Artforum*, New York, June 1973

Frank, Peter. "Manifestations internationales: New York — Hans Haacke", *arTitudes*, No. 5, Paris, June/July/August 1973

Haacke, Hans. In "*The Role of the Artist in Today's Society — A Symposium at Oberlin*," Supplement Allen Memorial Art Museum Bulletin, Vol. XXX, No.3, Oberlin College, 1973 (reprinted in *Art Journal*, New York, Summer 1975)

Battcock, Gregory. "New York", *Arts Magazine*, New York, August 1973

Stitelman, Paul. "New York Galleries", *Arts Magazine*, New York, November 1973

Anderson, Laurie. "Ten Artists (John Weber Gallery)", *Art News*, New York, November 1973

1974

Haacke, Hans. "Profile", *Studio International*, London, February 1974

Perreault, John. "It says so on the door!", *The Village Voice*, New York, March 28, 1975

Kuhn, Annette. "Culture Shock", *The Village Voice*, New York, March 28, 1974

Albright, Thomas. "Hans Haacke's Work is 'Another Level of Reality' ", *San Francisco Chronicle*, March 30, 1974

Olson, Roberta J.M. "Live!", *Arts Magazine*, New York, May 1974

Haacke, Hans. "Manet-PROJEKT'74", *EXTRA*, No. 1, Cologne, July 1974

Stachelhaus, Heiner. "Kunstkrach um ein Gemälde von Manet aus dem Jahre 1880 — 'Spargelstilleben' mit Hermann J. Abs", *Neue Rhein-Zeitung*, Düsseldorf, July 4, 1974

Plunien, Eo. "Viel Lärm um ein Spargelbündel", *Die Welt*, Hamburg, July 5, 1974

Ohff, Heinz. "Schwierigkeiten mit den siebziger Jahren", *Der Tagesspiegel*, Berlin, July 9, 1974

Jappe, Georg. "Kehrt die Kunst zum Publikum zurück?", *Frankfurter Allgemeine Zeitung*, Frankfurt, July 10, 1974

Glozer, Laszlo. "Das Museum umarmt die Avantgarde", *Süddeutsche Zeitung*, München, July 10, 1974

Staeck, Klaus. "Der Leimtopf als Argument", *Der Tagesspiegel*, Berlin, July 12, 1974

Krüger, Werner. "Bemerkungen — Briefe, Vorwürfe, Krach", *Kölner Stadtanzeiger*, Cologne, July 13/14, 1974

Hohmeyer, Jürgen. "Kunst auf der Kippe", *Der Spiegel*, Hamburg, July 15, 1974

Plunien, Eo. "Der Kulturbetrieb gebar eine Maus", *Die Welt*, Hamburg, July 16, 1974

Trappschuh, Elke. " 'Spurensuche' nach der Verbindlichkeit der Kunst", *Handelsblatt*, Düsseldorf, August 13, 1974

"Projekt '74 (Kunst bleibt Kunst)". *Data*, Milan, Vol. IV, No. 12, Summer 1974

Haacke, Hans. "Manet-PROJEKT'74, sulla censura del Wallraf-Richartz-Museum al suo lavoro per Project'74", *Data*, Vol. IV, No. 12, Milan, Summer 1974

Tomič, Biljana. On Projekt'74 in *Moment*, No. 4, Belgrade, Summer 1974

Harrison, Charles and Morris, Lynda. "Review 6 — Projekt'74", *Studio International*, London, September 1974

Macaire, Alain. "Cologne — Projekt'74", *+ − 0*, No. 5,

Brussels, September 1974

Honnef, Klaus. "Projekt'74 a Colonia", *Domus,* Milan, September 1974

Frank, Peter. "Reviews, Art Now-Projekt", *Architecture Plus,* New York, Sept./Oct. 1974

"Actualité", *Art Press,* No. 13, Paris, Sept./Oct. 1974

Haacke, Hans. Untitled catalogue text in *Art into Society – Society into Art,* Institute of Contemporary Arts, London, 1974

Tisdall, Caroline. "In this country the role allocated to art is still mostly that of the incidental pleasure-giver . . . Real events in Germany have ruled out this complacency", *The Guardian,* London, November 1, 1974

Vaisey, Marina. "Drawing the Lessons of History", *The Sunday Times,* London, November 3, 1974

Cork, Richard. "The Real Life Brigade", *Evening Standard,* London, November 7, 1974

Overy, Paul. "Should Artists go on Strike?", *The Times,* London, November 12, 1974

Baldwin, Carl R. "Haacke: Refusé in Cologne", *Art in America,* New York, November 1974

Haacke, Hans. "Manet-PROJEKT'74", *Avalanche,* New York, December 1974

Buren, Daniel and Bear, Liza. "Daniel Buren . . . Kunst Bleibt Politik", *Avalanche,* New York, December 1974

1975

Haacke, Hans. "Solomon R. Guggenheim Museum Board of Trustees", *TRI-Quarterly,* No. 32, Winter 1975, Northwestern University, Evanston, Ill.

Morris, Lynda. "Art into Society: Society into Art, Seven German Artists, at the I.C.A., London", *Studio International,* London, Jan./Feb. 1975

Burnham, Jack. "Meditations on a Bunch of Asparagus", *Arts Magazine,* New York, February 1975

Joachimides, Christos. "Art into Society — Society into Art", *Kunstforum,* Mainz, Vol. 13, Feb./Apr. 1975

Teyssedre, Bernard. "L'art sociologique", *Opus International,* Paris, No. 55, April 1975

Da Vinci, Mona. "More Than Meets the Eye", *The Soho Weekly News,* New York, May 22, 1975

Beaucamp, Eduard. "Avantgarde im Glockenturm", *Frankfurter Allgemeine Zeitung,* Frankfurt, June 2, 1975

Davis, Douglas. "Spring Fashions", *Newsweek,* New York, June 2, 1975

Burnham, Jack. "Hans Haacke's Seurat Exhibition: The Perils of Radicalism", *New Art Examiner,* Chicago, June 1975

Ramsden, Mel. "Perimeters of Protest", *The Fox,* New York, Vol. 1, No. 1, 1975

André, Michael. "New York Reviews", *Art News,* New York, Sept. 1975

Heineman, Susan. "Reviews: Hans Haacke, John Weber Gallery", *Artforum,* New York, Sept. 1975

Kozloff, Max. "Painting and Anti-Painting: a Family Quarrel", *Artforum,* New York, Sept. 1975

Gordon, Mary. "Art and Politics—Five Interviews with: Carl Baldwin, Hans Haacke, Alice Neel, May Stevens, Leon Golub," *STRATA,* School of Visual Arts, New York, Vol. 1, No. 1, 1975.

Collins, Tara. "Hans Haacke", *Arts Magazine,* New York, October 1975

Jack Burnham

Steps in the Formulation of Real-Time Political Art

The Early Works and Their Context:

In comparison to other contemporary artists, Hans Haacke's work finds itself uniquely balanced between American and European post-formalist art. His early water boxes, the condensation cubes, free-floating balloons, sails, and freezing constructions reveal a direct affinity to New Tendency/Zero esthetics in Europe (ca. 1956-68). One could sense at that time a budding counter-movement to the prevailing mannerisms of painterliness and decorative expressionism. What some artists in Düsseldorf, Paris, and Milan substituted for these exhausted mannerisms was a rigorous use of actual movement, motif repetition, and literal surfaces; they chose the phenomenological emphasis to the formal idiom.

We can perceive in Haacke's works of this period, metaphysical links with Jean Tinguely's machines, and also with Yves Klein's transmogrification of the elements of nature. Haacke's year in Paris (1960-61) was also valuable in that he came in contact with the magnetic sculptures of the Greek artist Takis. In Düsseldorf, near Haacke's home city of Cologne, Otto Piene, Heinz Mack, and Günther Uecker held a number of exhibitions (1957-63) under the title of *Group Zero*. Shadows, raised reliefs, reflective surfaces, artificial lighting and night-time spectaculars played a major role in *Zero*'s plastic principles. Some of these ideas were revived from constructivist and Bauhaus pedagogy of the 1920's.

In the early 1960's Haacke was included in a number of important Zero exhibitions (e.g., in London, Ulm, Amsterdam, Berlin, Venice, and Washington D.C.). On the strength of some success in Europe, Haacke returned to New York City in the spring of 1965, and with an American wife. He had lived with a Fulbright Scholarship in Philadelphia and New York from 1961 to 1963. The situation had changed so that many of the plastic aspects of New Tendency/Zero art were very much in vogue, although it continued to remain in direct opposition to the prevailing forces of American "mainstream" formalist painting and sculpture. Yet, in Haacke's work, there seemed to be an austerity and

quasi-functionalism that gave it a passing resemblance to American Minimalism. As Minimalism developed during the early 1960's, it was Haacke's dual role as a citizen of West Germany and an alien resident of the United States that brought him into direct proximity with both alternatives to Formalism.

The political spectrum surrounding the type of work with which Haacke sympathised in Europe during the 1960's was conflicting and confusing. It ranged from Zero's liberalism to the decidedly more leftist position of the Parisian *Groupe de recherche d'art visuel*. Among the latter for example the Argentinian Le Parc was temporarily deported for his political activism during the May events of 1968. He was also among the most vocal agitators in 1972 against participation in the so-called Expo Pompidou organized at the request of the French President to celebrate 10 years of French Contemporary Art. Neo-dadaists, such as Jean Tinguely, never hid their sympathy for nihilism and anarchism; in part we might suspect a revolt against the quiet orderliness of Swiss life. Hungarian-born Victor Vasarely wrote several social tracts and art manifestos in the preceding decade that bear the influence of socialist theory. Among other things, they advocated low-cost multiple editions long before these became fashionable. While writing polemics attacking artists whose single goal is fame and money, Vasarely has become one of the richest artists in Europe. There are the scientism and socio-experimental theories of the cybernetic artist, Nicolas Schoeffer, and that of the *Groupe de recherche d'art visuel* (founded in 1960). Neither ever fused his or their goals into a specific and workable social plan, but instead their energies have been drained off by high-art consumerism. Much the same is true for the members of *Group Zero* and allied European groups; early idealism tended to degenerate into chic interior decoration.

In the early 1960's, several New Tendency exhibitions were organized in Zagreb by the Yugoslav Marxist critic, Matko Mestrović. In a declaration written in 1963 in conjunction with several artists from Paris,

Meštrović insisted that a "progressive" abstract art is possible, certainly a "revisionist" position to take vis-à-vis orthodox Socialist Realism.[1] Allied groups, particularly those in Milan and Poland, supported the move towards experimental objectivity, anonymity, perceptual psychology, and socialism — while other groups such as *Zero* and *NUL* from Holland took the path towards individual expression, poetic idealism, and abstract immateriality.

Fifteen years earlier in the United States, the possibility of a viable political art faded with the decline of regionalist realism and the shift of previously Marxist critics and artists in the New York area to a position of abstraction for its own sake. Perhaps it must be conceeded that the appearance of Abstract Expressionism was a strategic god-send during the period of rampant McCarthyism and an equally active House Committee on Un-American Activities (ca. 1947-1956).

In retrospect, the early Russian Constructivists — Tatlin, Malevich, Gabo, and Lissitzky — were ardent sympathizers with the first phases of the Bolshevik Revolution, but gradual disillusionment led each of them variously into mysticism, industrial design, and Western gallery commerce. Under the circumstance, one might well ask why artists with leftist attitudes should so often be drawn towards non-objective esthetics. Certainly the doctrines of Marxist-Leninism forbid abstraction in all of its forms as a part of the cult of bourgeois elitism. Looking towards Germany with the rise of Hitler, and to the United States during the 1930's and '40's, one remembers that abstractionist esthetics were always a favorite target of rightist politicians, and also of the less educated bourgeoisie. Inasmuch as non-objective painting represented the spearhead of avant-gardism, it remained "revolutionary" and left-of-center in international art circles — or at least this was so until a few years ago. Nevertheless, the "messages" and meta-language assumptions of non-objective painting remained vaguely emotional and legendary, addressing themselves primarily to psychic shifts within the narrowing confines of the Art World. We might reasonably assume that non-objective art has already reached a point of culmination. Both the New Tendency in Europe and American Formalism remained clearly incapable of addressing themselves to any issue except their status as ideas about art vis-à-vis other existing ideas about art.

As a close friend of Hans Haacke since 1962, I observed how the idea of allowing his "systems" to take root in the real world began to fascinate him, more and more, almost to a point of obsession. He sensed that his systems were in essence still objects, still vulnerable to the formalist games of visual indulgence and delectation. And I think he sensed that he had to move towards *terra incognita*. A letter from him during the Spring of 1968 describes the opening of the

Plus by Minus: Today's 1/2 Century exhibition in Buffalo, New York. In a sense, it represents his summation of a tradition.

> The Buffalo show is very strange, so strange, that I cannot really say that it is good or bad. There were some beautiful old examples of things that are known only from books, and even some items whose existence I had no idea of at all. I was very excited about Malevich's pencil drawings of 1913: squares and a single circle. Also a small wooden Vantongerloo and the Medunetzky sculpture in Camilla Gray's book. And also Lissitzky drawings, and Taeuber-Arp, and the de Stijl with some rarely shown examples, Bill, Lohse and many more. All the people I've mentioned present a fantastic depth of concept and conviction. What was so strange was the juxtaposition with contemporary, related (?) works. The contemporary pieces look both frivolous as well as more at ease, less dusty, less contrived, less like coming out of a study. There was obviously a tremendous gap, and all factors taken into consideration it was hard to take sides for either of the two (?) generations. Contemporary work also seemed to be less sectarian, so much so that it becomes questionable if one can construe something like a direct line from "constructivism" to minimal and related works. Disregarding the formalist aspects, like hard-edge, industrial materials, impersonal working methods, etc., it is very hard to say if Bob Morris should not be equally grouped with the surrealists. And there are others who do not necessarily fit into the tight-assed history of constructivism. I myself have very mixed feelings about my own heritage. Duchamp seems to be as important as Malevich or Mondrian. I certainly have nothing to do with the Gabo wing. Gabo's retrospective was a disaster! I subscribe to every word Hilton Kramer wrote about it in the *Times,* although I am not a fan of his, as you know. With the exception of the celluloid heads and some string plastic constructions he is a cornball *par excellence*. Perhaps I have to admit that some of the models for architecture and his project for an open air light show at the Brandenburg gate should be taken seriously. But so much is not thought out to its logical conclusion and plays with science fiction imagery. Worst of all the paintings on motorized discs, a terrible embarrassment. Next to all these ghastly things the work of his colleagues in Russia looks so much more gutsy and adventurous, even his brother looks better in comparison.[2]

It is evident from other letters of that period that Haacke was becoming very wary of the chic superficiality that surrounded so many of the kinetic performances and "light events" in which he at first so willingly participated. There was, in fact, more than a little of the uptown discotheque in Haacke's gallery, Howard Wise. A letter of his recounts the installation of the Air Art exhibition put on by Willoughby Sharp in the spring of 1968.

> . . . an hour before the opening tables and chairs were moved into the well-composed installation in preparation for the party. Soon everyone was smashed out of his skull. People were throwing foam around from Medalla's *Cloud Canyon*. The patroness danced over my white flow-piece and had a ball, other works were treated like fun-house furniture. Drinks made a profit of $300 — $10 worth of catalogues were sold, and the place was a mess! Willoughby did not attend the party given in his honor afterwards. I could be cynical now and ask, is it for this public that I am making an effort to become a popular success? I am reminded of the Tennessee museum curator who called the gallery [Howard Wise] a little while ago, asking for an artist to give a happening at the end of his inauguration dinner at the museum. There remains a great demand for court jesters.[3]

Haacke's Political Growth

In reading over Haacke's letters before 1968 I was struck by the absence of political remarks, although Haacke has always impressed me as a keenly political being. Compared to most artists, Haacke's reading interests remain abnormally large. He has an addiction for news periodicals, *Der Spiegel* and *The New York Times* being always at hand. Haacke's emotional energies are periodically directed by current news events and how they fit into his particular world-view. Political art as such has rarely interested Haacke, usually, I suspect, because of its laboredness and predictability. He maintains that Socialist Realism had nothing to offer.

Haacke lived as a child with his parents in Cologne and in a suburb of the city of Bonn. He retains memories of the period of World War II when he was 3 to 9 years old. His parents were anti-Nazi; his father was a member of the Social Democratic Party as a youth and he later became a follower of Antroposophy, a synthesis of mystical beliefs banned by the Nazis. His father lost his job with the City of Cologne because he was not prepared to join the Nazi Party. Survival under such circumstances meant that Haacke was taught from his earliest years to be completely discrete about his family's views among his school friends and with adults. This has engendered in Haacke a certain natural secretiveness and anonymity. Haacke still refuses either to sign his art works or to allow photographs to be taken of him. Given the American mania for publicity particularly in the arts, sports and politics,

this appears somewhat odd, something on the order of a phobia. However, the objective and anonymous character of his work almost demands it, and this is particularly true of the later political pieces.

Still, it is obvious to anyone mildly familiar with the gallery promotion system that the art magazines and media publicity are its life-blood. So the fact that the name "Haacke" commands a certain amount of attention, in part through the artist's news making confrontations with public institutions — provides a nice sense of irony. It is ironic since Haacke's art seems to be most effective when it generates a public confrontation, one which personalizes the inherent contradictions between the institution's values and Haacke's function as a social critic.

Haacke's willingness to bring social issues to the public's attention, may in part be due to his year in Paris after he finished art school (1960-61). At the time he had the opportunity to witness police reprisals against students, intellectuals, and Leftists who marched in protest against French colonial policies in Algeria. Involved as he was on the edges of these sometimes violent demonstrations, it seemed obvious that the police were organized into para-military squads so as to protect, not the civil order, but the interests of the white Algerians.

During the spring of 1968, Haacke closely followed the May Revolution. In essence it was a rebellion by the New Left against the "consumer society." This was spear-headed, not by the French Communist Party or the labor unions, but by bourgeois students in colleges in and around Paris. Students of the École des Beaux-Arts organized themselves into the "Atelier Populaire", the studio mainly responsible for posters, murals, and street theatre during the May Revolution. It brought to light the contradictions implicit in the role of a middle-class avant-garde artist. Once examined and stripped of its rhetorical glow, "creative freedom" amounts to an artist being able to manipulate colors and forms to his heart's content. As the Atelier Populaire stated in their position paper of May 21st, 1968,

1. He [the artist] does what he wants to do, he believes that everything is possible, he is accountable only to himself or to Art.
2. He is a "creator" which means that out of all things he invents something that is unique, whose value will be permanent and beyond historical reality. He is not a worker at grips with historical reality. The idea of creation gives his work an unreal quality. In giving him this privileged status, culture puts the artist in a position where he can do no harm and in which he functions as a safety-valve in the mechanism of bourgeois society.[4]

1 *Condensation Cube,* 1963/65

2 *Live Airborne System*, 1965/68

For Haacke, as for many of us, the Vietnam War provided a long and debilitating exposure to the near futility of trying to change a nation's policies — even as the existing policies proved to be grossly wasteful and immoral. Collectively, it generated a vast degree of frustration which had no effective outlet. Artist committees, rallies, and petition-signing were token efforts which only gained in effectiveness as they became nation-wide. At the occasion of Martin Luther King's assassination, he writes in a letter dated April 10th, 1968,

Last week's murder of Dr. King came as a great shock. Linda [his wife] and I were gloomy for days and still have not quite recovered. The event pressed something into focus that I have known for long but never realized so bitterly and helplessly, namely, that what we are doing, the production and the talk about sculpture, has no relation to the urgent problems of our society. Whoever believes that art can make life more humane is utterly naive. Mondrian was one of those naive saints. . . . Nothing, but really absolutely nothing is changed by whatever type of painting or sculpture or happening you produce on the level where it counts, the political level. Not a single napalm bomb will not be dropped by all the shows of ''Angry Arts''. Art is utterly unsuited as a political tool. No cop will be kept from shooting a black by all the light-environments in the world. As I've said, I've known that for a number of years and I was never really bothered by it. All of a sudden it bugs me. I am also asking myself, why the hell am I working in this field at all. Again an answer is never at hand that is credible, but it did not particularly disturb me. I still have no answer, but I am no longer comfortable.[5]

During the fall of 1969, Haacke, with numbers of other New York artists, became involved in a movement which soon defined itself as the Art Workers Coalition (1969-72). As a professional group, fine artists are probably the least organized and, in some cases, the most exploited. They have virtually no collective control over social and economic policy within their field. The Art Workers Coalition was an initial recognition of this situation, and as was to be expected, it generated a great deal of rhetoric but very little in the way of concrete accomplishments. Of its demands to the Museum of Modern Art, only the free day once a week to visitors was granted, and this has since been diluted by requiring an entrance fee in whatever amount the public chooses to pay. Prolonged labor disputes between the professional staff below the rank of curator and the Museum of Modern Art's administration erupted a little later, possibly spurred by the consciousness raising example of the Art Workers Coalition. In part because of his own related projects, Haacke maintained close liaison with the leaders of the strikes at the Modern.

Possibly one of the important political catalysts for Haacke's decision to expand his systems art was the general boycott by artists of the 10th Sao Paulo Bieñal in Brazil during the summer of 1969. In March of 1969 Gyorgy Kepes, Director of the Center for Advanced Visual Studies at M.I.T. in Cambridge was approached by representatives of the U.S. Government to organize the American entry for the Bieñal. Kepes and the Fellows at the Center agreed and proceeded to invite artists not affiliated with the Center, Haacke among them. But within a few weeks a "pullout" from the Bieñal of international proportions was underway

3 *Grass Grows,* 1967/69

4 *Circulation,* 1969

in protest against the repressive nature of the military dictatorship ruling Brazil.

By early summer *The New York Times* had reported that *two* French delegations withdrew from the Bieñal; E. de Wilde, director of the Amsterdam Stedelijk Museum, pulled out his selection of Dutch artists; Pontus Hulten did the same for Swedish artists, and other names gradually added to this mounting number. Gyorgy Kepes had no intention of abandoning the Bieñal, instead, he and the Fellows, with a few notable exceptions, regarded it as an opportunity to communicate "vital, progressive ideas" to a country ridden with "inhuman political processes".[7] In a letter, the critic Dore Ashton, then in France, stated that she was not surprised by Kepes' response. She goes on to say

I would have said, could I have written a protest, that the persistence of American intellectuals in the essentially egoistic belief that "exchange" is so good for those poor benighted provincials is really almost criminal. *Whom* are they going to communicate with? *My* friends [meaning Brazilian friends] are either in exile or under house arrest![8]

Kepes and the Fellows at the Center responded to Dore Ashton's argument by pointing out that in most instances the dissenting artists would not be adverse to representing the United States in an exhibition staged in a Communist Country. The reply to this argument was that the opposition was primarily directed against the tacit support of a policy whereby the U.S. State Department continues to aid and encourage right-wing dictatorships. Earlier in April, Haacke drove this point home to me in a letter that followed a meeting that he had with Kepes in New York.

After I left Kepes I became haunted by the thoughts that I have expressed to you about being an accom-

plice of the U.S. Government—if I participate in a show under its auspices abroad. I finally have decided not to show and just wrote a letter to that effect to Kepes.

I believe any exhibition organized and in the name of the U.S. Government abroad is a public relations job for this government and has the potential to divert attention from its machinations and the war in Vietnam. It is the old fig-leaf story. Unfortunately we are not living in a time when art (whatever that is) can be seen and shown simply as what it is. Repressive tolerance diverts the information and makes it into a U.S.I.A. stunt. It is just obscene to play innocent, particularyly in a show organized for a country whose regime lives by the grace of the C.I.A..

As you know I am no purist in these matters. I do show in galleries, museums, etc.. . . With all these examples you are naturally dealing in one way or another with the establishment through money that was made on the war and with the commercialization of art. However, in none of these cases did I officially represent U.S. policies. I take advantage of a situation that I have not created, as well as I can (I am not very efficient at it). And I have no qualms about living on war money, it would be there to be spent anyhow. . . .[9]

General System Theory:

From 1965 to the present Haacke has identified his art with ideas implicit to General Systems Theory. In part, he has employed systems thinking to disassociate himself from the intentions of formalist art. Rather than the manipulation of color, gestalts and textured surfaces, he has chosen to define his art in terms of open and closed systems, self-regulating, as opposed to run-a-way systems, and hierarchical organization of physical relationships. Concerning his condensation cubes, he writes, "I was very excited about the subtle communication with a seemingly sealed off environment and the complexity of interrelated conditions determining a meteorological process."[10]

In works dealing with the natural elements, decisions as to shape, color, composition, texture, and spatial arrangement were decided according to practical considerations of fabrication — these in turn tended to clarify the systems involved. The systemic notion of internal and external boundaries reflects the idea of a "dialectics of transformation." In regard to this, he speaks of the "independence" of his systems as self-sustaining functioning entities. Yet their fine arts context allows them to share the cultural overtones of their environment. According to Haacke, this produces in the viewer's mind a condition of conceptual oscillation. Thus his art may be seen for its active participation with the environment (e.g. as an ongoing physical process or as a socio-economic indicator), or it may be construed as "art" in dialectical conflict with previous art. For Haacke, this irresolution remains of prime importance.

Systems analysis is largely a technique developed after World War II for organizational purposes; to some extent it remains an offshoot of General Systems Theory. Haacke is quick to acknowledge his debt to the founder (in the 1920's) of General Systems Theory, the biologist, Ludwig von Bertalanffy. Some of Haacke's thinking derives from Bertalanffy's summation of his philosophy in his book, *General Systems Theory* (1968).[11] While it in turn has been labeled "functionalistic" by some of its critics, Bertalanffy's thinking represents a major departure from the mechanistic biology and physics of the past fifty years. The strength of systems theory has been its goal of hierarchically linking all levels of animate and inanimate nature, but it remains weak in its ability to define broad-spectrum equations which correspond to these divergent levels of nature. Beginning with static and purely mechanical structure, Bertalanffy sees man's symbolic systems (e.g., language, mathematics, logic, art, music, etc.) as spanning the upper ranges of the systems hierarchy. These, in fact, bear a complexity which extends throughout all nature by analogy. Thus high levels presuppose the organization of lower levels. Haacke is attracted by Bertalanffy's ability to see isomorphisms between different fields and at different levels of systemic complexity.

Bertalanffy has shown that every living thing is by nature an *open system;* hence it sustains itself by an inflow and outflow of materials and energy, so that it constantly builds, destroys, and rebuilds its own structure. This metabolic exchange between a system and its environment produces chemical, thermodynamic and informational stability. Open systems with their flexible and inflexible boundaries, represent life itself. The significance of some of Haacke's political pieces lies in his ability to break down boundaries of existing art relationships. There is a double bind in his strategy. Haacke is producing a fresh and perhaps historically inevitable art just as he is undermining the institutions responsible for the selling or collecting of fine art. Part of the esthetic of his art is to reveal the ideological and economic underpinnings of a given culture or to create conditions in which these reveal themselves. And it is in a parallel sense that Bertalanffy describes one of the paradoxes inherent in all living systems:

> In this contrast between wholeness and sum lies the tragical tension in any biological, psychological and sociological evolution. Progress is possible only by passing from a state of undifferentiated wholeness to differentiation of parts. This implies, however, that the parts become fixed with respect to a certain action. Therefore, progressive segregation also means progressive mechanization. Progressive mechanization, however, implies loss of regulability. As long as a system is a unitary whole, a disturbance will be followed by the attainment of a new stationary state, due to the interactions within the system. The system is self-regulating. If, however, the system is split up into independent causal chains, regulability disappears. The partial processes will go on irrespective of each other.[12]

Over a century ago, the novelist Gustave Flaubert wrote, "The more that art develops the more scientific it must be, just as science will become esthetic." This and quotes similar to it received considerable attention in the art magazines during the last decade. For a time, even, it held promise of coming true. The notion of a

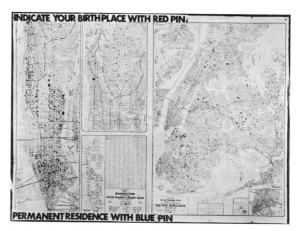

5 *Gallery-Goers' Birthplace and Residence Profile, Part 1,* 1969. Excerpt

"Systems Esthetics" appeared to have validity as momentum built up for Earth Art, Ecological Art, Body Art, Video Art, and the multitudinous forms of Conceptualism. It became also evident that what we nominally regard as the "Art World," with its various adjuncts of gallery, museum, and media support, is, in fact, a specific set of systemic relationships with many of the features of a living organism.

In part because of the peculiar publicity that systems thinking has received, we tend to hold to the attitude that it is a unique tool of the giant corporations, military think-tanks, and the Pentagon. For much of the Art World techniques that threaten to explain or reveal social structures and social myths are regarded with suspicion or hostility — even as they are practiced by artists within the milieu. Given the fact that sociological analysis of the Art World is scant and difficult to come by, no sufficient reason has even been brought forth as to why so much of its population is, by and large, Liberal to Radical Left in its political leanings. Such a spectrum of attitudes would normally tend to regard "systems analysis," or any derived discipline, as a failed techno-ideology of the Right, e.g., as the military-industrial strategy of the Vietnam War meant to "solve" mega-dollar problems in logistics and weaponry; semicolor instead it seemed to have been proven that "man" (i.e., "spirit") still may triumph over "technology" (i.e., "matter"). Yet, in spite of this expropriation, or misappropriation, the systems approach appears to be a neutral scientific tool, one that has already made deep inroads into the social sciences, engineering, architecture, industry, and the more liberal concerns of conservation, pollution control, wild-life ecology, and human demography. On a broad level, it begins as a means of dividing up very desperate "problems":

6 *Gallery Goers' Residence Profile, Part 2,* 1970. View of Installation

1. Determinants: elements outside the operating system itself which determine the nature, form, and limits of the system. These include such items as general and specific statements of the system's purpose, inputs from other systems, and the constraints of all sorts which place bounds upon the system.
2. Components: the "moving parts" of the system, which include the mechanisms, men, and facilities within the system.
3. System Integrators: elements that integrate the moving parts. These include "operating sequences, communications, organization, and decision structure.[13]

The ostensible purpose of this technique is to organize problem criteria, and in doing so to correct poor existing design, resource imbalances, and inefficiency. But as one professor of Business Administration has observed in a critique of the systems approach,[14] a society's goals are relativistic, shifting as they do from one social stratum to the next. The question rapidly becomes, "what stratum of the social hierarchy dominates our systems perspective?" Regardless of the supposed objectivity of the systems approach, it remains a formalistic problem-solving device with, as a rule, implicit points of view, which are usually the result of political direction.

The term "real-time" is a concept that was first developed in the late 1950's and early 1960's by the designers of the computer systems network for the United States Air Force Strategic Air Command. Their goal was to develop a world-wide monitoring network that would provide minute-to-minute response to any sign of a missile or bomber attack, or even an air-incursion, at any point on the globe. Gradually the term "real-time" has been applied to time-sharing computer systems where there is no more than a normal conversational interval between a computer and its user. In other words, the computer responds at a rate of speed which is not too different from that used by persons engaged in normal conversation. Traditionally, art works exist in "mythical time," that is in an ideal historical time-frame separated from the day-to-day events of the real world. Some systems and conceptual artists, such as Haacke, attempt to integrate their works into the actual events of the "real world," that is the world of politics, money-making, ecology, industry, and other pursuits. In effect, the work becomes not only the original concept or piece, but any significant public or official response to it, or any further variations which the work may take as a result of its engagement with the world-at-large.

As an extension of the real-time systems concept, Haacke's works quite often bear a resemblance to Marcel Duchamp's Ready-mades. Like Duchamp,

Haacke employs everyday objects in his art. Often their meanings are inverted or heightened by their usage in a gallery or museum. But unlike Duchamp, Haacke's assemblies of functional objects and conventions continue operating in their normal way and are not meant to be baffling or esoteric. Their purposes are generally apparent. Haacke has used teletype machines, refrigeration machinery, chicken incubators, polling devices, and sewage-filtering equipment in a relatively straightforward manner. His surveys and provenances through the use of certain type faces, thin black frames, wide margins, and de-

7 *On Sale at the Foundation Maeght,* Excerpt of manuscript for performance

8 *Turtles Set Free,* June 20, 1970

sign austerity gain the look and the "feeling" of real documents. In the case of his engraved magnesium plaques with quotations by American businessmen and politicians, there is a sense of solemnity and commemoration fitting a corporation lobby or board room.

Systems and Social Evolution

Social and scientific theories reside on two levels: as formal theory and as a working infra-structure which, to some extent, may mirror structural properties of the theory. The same is true of art theory and its social expression. In time we may come to the conclusion that modern formalist art (art which is appreciated primarily for its devices of color, texture, and composition) is analogically equivalent to various forms of art traffic originating in the 19th Century. Such art may bear underlying comparison to the rise of commercial art galleries and the private acquisition of large and valuable collections for public display. Inasmuch as these have served a valuable historical function as repositories for past art, they sustain the sacred ethos behind the art impulse as a mechanical determination of class relationships. In essence policy-making remains the province of the financially most powerful. Participation in art's social affairs is limited to select groups, while only the viewing of artifacts, as these have been determined by the museum's hierarchy, is open to the public. We may enter a period when the mechanical devices of upper-middle class art consumerism, a manipulated art market, and vast public art collections, may become functionally and financially inoperable, and may, in fact, be vestiges of the past. These will gradually appear anachronistic and, as Bertalanffy states in a more general context, the art impulse will become progressively fragmented, a series of differentiated areas, each reflecting its own internal contradictions. Each area of the art impulse will function paradoxically, implying a wholeness which is lacking within the existing social order. One suspects that as art's "utilitarian function" imperceptibly disappears, that is, as its psycho-therapeutic and pedagogical properties bring less and less satisfaction to the public at large, there will be more attempts to academically reinstitute the tenets of "valid art," and to bring contemporary art into line with the conserving values of society. By its nature, art is *organic,* which means that is is free neither of material or mechanistic constraints but that it has the desire to transcend these limitations. Whether art's constraining forces are American businessmen or Russian commissars, ultimately they succeed only in suppressing the cathartic and liberating value of art as a vehicle for social evolution.

To Haacke's credit, he has penetrated the normalizing facade of laissez-faire surrounding the socio-economic activities of the Art World, and he has ren-

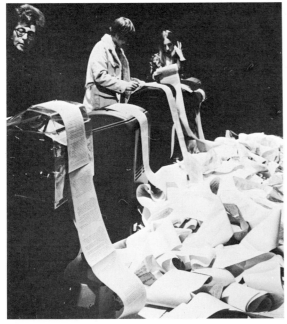

9 *News,* 1969/70

dered "visible" what has been up to now structurally "invisible." His work attacks the values of consumer art in a free market system, while never relinquishing its status as a consumer product itself. Vital art, in terms of Bertalanffy's General Systems Theory, gives equal value to life and death, maintenance and change. The free market is a functionalist device, a philosophy of pragmatic trade relationships which clings to the "pratical," the "life-sustaining," and "raw survival" as ends in themselves; because its goals are survival and growth at all costs, they embody the seeds of their own destruction. In Bertalanffy's words,

> The main critique of functionalism . . . is that it overemphasizes maintenance, equilibrium, adjustment, homeostasis, stable institutional structures, and so on, with the result that history, process, sociocultural change, inner-directed development, etc., are underplayed and, at most, appear as "deviants" with a negative value connotation. The theory therefore appears to be one of conservatism and conformism, definding the "system" . . . . as is, conceptually neglecting and hence obstructing social change.[15]

Ultimately the "thingification" of art and by that I mean all tendencies which seek to enclose, manipulate, objectify, seduce, and expropriate the art impulse ends by generating entropy and institutional decay within the structures which have heretofore "preserved" art. If we look below the surface of Haacke's art, he is neither subverting nor undermining the art object, but simply revealing to us its true *after-life*. As inflexible and philosophically pedestrian as institutionalized Marxism appears to many of us in the West today, we must remember that Karl Marx had a very real appreciation for the near mystical transubstantiation of consumer objects through their phases of development.

> A commodity appears at first sight, a very trivial thing, and easily understood. Analysis shows that it is in reality a very peculiar thing, abounding in metaphysical subtleties and theological niceties.[16]

The philosopher Friedrich Hegel, before Marx, also understood the process whereby utilitarian objects, as well as art works, ultimately mirror human alienation. In fact, it is the very formalistic abstractness of the art object in its later stages which concurrently transforms the artist into a formal object. For all the lionizing and fraternization famous artists receive at the convenience of wealthy patrons and museum officials, few of them are naive enough to forget their status as favored objects of the moment, more properly as extensions of their art. One of the minor purposes of Haacke's political works is to alienate the rich and powerful from their own art commodities, thus dialectically reversing the process of confusing human beings with objects. It is apparent that often the motivations of collectors become the material for Haacke's work.

Observations on the Political Works:

A point of focus for Haacke's first political art was his *Gallery-Goers' Birthplace and Residence Profile* at the Howard Wise Gallery, New York, during November of 1969. Visitors were requested to mark with pins their place of birth and present residence on large-scale maps of New York City, the area within 50-miles of New York, the United States and the world. This piece was extended by a series of photographs taken at all locations marked as residences with pins on the Manhattan map which was exhibited at the Paul Maenz Gallery, Cologne, in January of 1971. For Haacke, it was revealing just how closely confined the gallery-going "Art World" really is. This and subsequent polls proved that it represents a relatively narrow spectrum of professional and economic interests.

There is also Haacke's Rockefeller Poll for which the question was given to the curator of the "Information" show only the very night before the opening. Haacke suspects that the Museum of Modern Art never appreciated the pointedness of his political question, but on the other hand their sense of public relations prevented them from making an issue over it. He noted that the poll served as a safety-valve for the political tempers of a surprisingly large number of museum visitors. The spring before, in 1969, he submitted several proposals to Maurice Tuchman for the "Art

214 E 3 St.
Block 385, lot 11
5 story walk-up old law tenement

Owned by Harpmel Realty, Inc., 608 E 11 St., NYC
Contracts signed by Harry J. Shapolsky, President(1963)
                    Martin Shapolsky, President(1964)
Principal Harry J. Shapolsky(according to Real Estate
Directory of Manhattan)

Acquired 8-21-1963 from John the Baptist Foundation,
c/o The Bank of New York, 48 Wall St., NYC,
for $237 600.- (also 7 other bldgs.)

$150 000.- mortgage at 6% interest, 8-19-1963, due
8-19-1968, held by The Ministers and Missionaries Benefit
Board of the American Baptist Convention,
475 Riverside Drive, NYC (also on 7 other bldgs.)

Assessed land value $25 000.-; total value $75 000.-
(including 212 and 216 E 3 St.), 1971

9 *Shapolsky et al Manhattan Real Estate Holdings, a Real-Time Social System, as of May 1, 1971,* Excerpt.

and Technology'' project (1967-1971) at the Los Angeles County Museum. He sent plans for several ''Wind'' and ''Cold-Warm'' environments, and also the most interesting proposal, ''Environmental Transplant.'' It consisted of a cylindrical room in the museum which was to receive, on a real-time basis, television images from a moving truck scanning Greater Los Angeles projecting them from a revolving projector onto the wall. This proved too complex and costly for the ''Art and Technology'' project, as did another work which was to be an ongoing computerized poll. Certainly the last two mentioned proposals have mild political overtones, and it became clear to Haacke that any museum could reject a proposal purely on a technological and cost basis and thereby use this as a smokescreen for their ideological bias. It also became apparent that art could be used to grease the ideological wheels of museums and businesses, his own works not excluded. Thus, he has since worked on the premise that all galleries and museums function under specific ideological constraints. He is careful though not to view these constraints in a mechanistic way as orthodox Marxists tend to do. In a statement of 1974 he explained,

> In principle, the decisions of museum officials, ideologically highly determined or receptive to deviations from the norm, follow the boundaries set by their employers. These boundaries need not be expressly stated in order to be operative. Frequently museum officials have internalized the thinking of their superiors to a degree that it becomes natural for them to make the ''right'' decisions and a congenial atmosphere reigns between employee and employer. Nevertheless it would be simplistic to assume that in each case museum officials are faithfully translating the interests of their superiors into museum policy, particularly since new cultural manifestations are not always recognizable as to their suitability or opposition to the parties concerned. The potential for confusion is increased by the fact that the convictions of an ''artist'' are not necessarily reflected in the objective position his/her work takes on the socio-political scale and that this position could change over the years to the point of reversal.[17]

Haacke has been questioned as to why he even bothers to show his work in a museum or gallery context since it appears to represent a negation of high art values, and to have more to do with various practical academic pursuits. His reply is that he sees the museum and gallery context as an absolutely necessary element for the meaning and functioning of his works; in other words, in his attempts to desacralize art, Haacke needs the dialectical foil of the art environment to provide the necessary contrast. For Haacke, a book of his polling results would provide little social weight in the art world. The questions had to be asked in the galleries and the gallery public had to be confronted with its "self-portrait" in that same environment. The walls of the museum or gallery are as much a part of his work as the items displayed on them. These works also need the "impregnation" of the gallery to set them in opposition to other contemporary art.

For the summer of 1970 he was invited by Dore Ashton to take part in an exhibition entitled "Art vivant américain" sponsored by the Fondation Maeght at St. Paul de Vence in the South of France. Haacke comments on the general conditions of the artists at the Fondation: "I got really pissed at M. Maeght because he treated the artists who were invited to do the work on their sites like dogs. He was incredibly arrogant — ending up dealing with the artists like his servants." On the other hand Haacke observes: "He [M. Maeght] visited Chagall every few days. Chagall had a villa up the road. Compared to Chagall, we were not in a price bracket where he felt he had to treat us like human beings."[18]

Possibly in opposition to the manicured environment at the Fondation Maeght Haacke produced some of his crudest and freest ecological works, simple gestures employing a goat, turtles, and wild vegetation. For an evening of performances, Haacke also structured a piece entitled *On Sale at the Fondation Maeght* in which a taped female voice announced the names of artists, titles, and prices of a series of original prints on sale at the bookstore of the Fondation Maeght, supposedly a non-profit organization. All the prints happened to be by artists shown regularly at the Galerie Maeght in Paris. Their aggregate value was over $190,000. These price quotations were regularly interrupted by a man reading over the telephone incoming teletype reports by Agence France Presse from the office of the local newspaper. The director of the Fondation attempted to halt the performance, but was unable to when he could not explain his reasons for doing so in public.

Five teletype machines were installed in the Jewish Museum of the "Software" exhibition during the Fall of 1970. These carried separate wire services and produced tons of raw news in the form of teletype paper every week. Thus the everyday political world, as filtered through the news agency entered the museum precinct.

The Guggenheim Affair

Shortly thereafter, Haacke was invited to prepare a one-man exhibition for the spring of 1971 at the Guggenheim Museum in New York City. With the curator, Edward Fry, Haacke decided on a presentation which would be divided into three parts: Physical Systems, Biological Systems, and Social Systems. The artist constructed new works for the show. Until a month and a half before the opening there was no question as to the validity or appropriateness of the works chosen. At that point the Director of the Museum, Thomas Messer, began to have serious doubts about allowing three Social Systems to be shown, one a visitor's poll and the others two complex pieces involving New York City real estate holdings. For some weeks, by letter and telephone, Haacke tried to arrive at a compromise with Messer which would satisfy the Director but would not dilute the integrity of the pieces. In late March it became evident that a compromise could not be reached. Messer publicly announced the cancellation of the exhibition, and Haacke took his case to the newspapers, television, and art magazines — the last being quite supportive. This did not prevent Messer from firing his curator, Edward Fry, when Fry took Haacke's side publicly and spoke of the dangers of censorship. To my knowledge it was the first time that an artist has carried his difficulties with a museum effectively into the mass media. As many have already observed, the ensuing controversy and public furor did more to focus upon Haacke and his work than half-a-dozen one-man exhibitions at the Guggenheim. If nothing else, Haacke proved that museums could no longer censor or reject artists' works — once a pro-

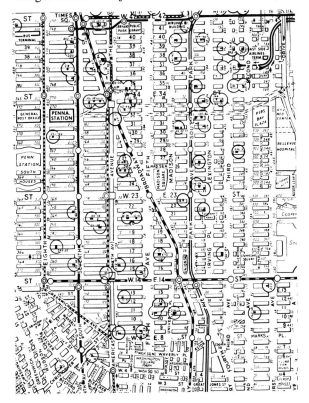

10 *Sol Goldman and Alex DiLorenzo Manhattan Real Estate Holdings, a Real-Time Social System, as of May 1, 1971*

posal is accepted for exhibition — on purely arbitrary grounds. Two of Haacke's incriminated pieces for that show were investigations of the holdings of two New York City real estate groups, one dealing primarily with slum properties, the other representing the largest private real estate conglomerate in all of Manhattan. With only public records at his disposal, Haacke traced the web of ownership for each of the real-estate groups, cross-indexing names of relatives, business associates, and dummy corporations. Each property was described by a photograph of the site, its address, the nominal legal owner, corporate officers, mortgages and their holders, the assessed value, and a large map showing their geographic location.

11 *Krefeld Sewage Triptych,* 1972.

12 *Rhine-Water Purification Plant ,* 1972

Thomas Messer, Director of the Guggenheim Museum, cancelled the exhibition on the grounds that it might engender legal action by the real estate operators. Also he felt that this work violated the political "neutrality" of the Guggenheim's charter as a public educational institution, reducing the museum to a forum for any and all political issues. In a guest editorial written for *Arts Magazine* in the June, 1971 issue, Messer makes the point that the Haacke-Guggenheim confrontation would have never taken place if they had relied upon the traditional system of selecting finished objects instead of relying on artists' proposals, the "improvisational working mode."[19] In other words, censorship remains undetected when a museum makes its decisions on completed art before announcing a public committment to the artist.

In the same editorial response to a prior editorial by Arts Magazine, Messer asserts that he never doubted Haacke's artistry but that

> To the degree to which an artist deliberately pursues aims that lie beyond art, his very concentration upon ulterior ends stands in conflict with the intrinsic nature of the work as an end in itself. The conclusion is that the sense of inappropriateness that was felt from the start toward Haacke's "social system" exhibit was due to an aesthetic weakness which interacted with a forcing of art boundaries. The tensions within this contradiction in the work itself transferred itself from it onto the museum environment and beyond it into society at large. Eventually, the choice was between the acceptance of or rejection of an alien substance that had entered the art museum organism."[20]

All this sounds strange indeed when one remembers the 19th and early 20th Century politically engaged artists, e.g., David, Géricault, Delacroix, Daumier, Courbet, Manet, Pissarro, Meunier, Tatlin, Rodchenko, Picasso, Heartfield, Kollwitz, Grosz, Siqueiros, and Rivera, to name the most prominent. Before the Solomon R. Guggenheim Museum's rise to power in the late 1950's we should remember that it was a *Museum of Nonobjective Art*, and that it was in part responsible for performing the "rites of purification" for the acceptance of avant-garde art into the American mainstream. This was first and foremost a content-free art, one allowing no "alien substance" to penetrate the Museum's sanctified environment. As Messer perceives, in the context of the Museum Haacke's work does present a "contradiction," but it is a contradiction which implicitly points towards the financial foundations of the Guggenheim itself, and this is what Messer cannot tolerate.

The anthropologist, Stanley Diamond, has written an insightful essay where he shows how Plato in his *Republic* stifles social "contradiction." The Republic, as Plato views it, maintains a highly structured class system and specialized divisions of labor. The citizen is bound to the State itself. Patriotism is the "royal lie" that raises the State above both the individual and his or her family. Only the poet, dramatist, or artist can deal with this collective fiction, as Plato knows too well. So he permits Socrates to give the following advice.

> When any one of these pantomimic gentlemen, who are so clever that they can imitate anything, come to us, and make a proposal to exhibit himself and his poetry, we will fall down and worship him as a sweet and holy and wonderful being; but we must also inform him that in our State such as he are not permitted to exist; the law will not allow them.[21]

Similarly, Thomas Messer informed the newspapers that: "Artistic merit was never a question. We invited him [Haacke] in the first place because we admire his work. I think that while the exposure of social malfunction is a good thing, it is not the function of a museum."[22]

Plato understood that all art contains an "ulterior motive" and is never "self-sufficient," as Messer stipulates, rather its self-sufficiency stems from the social approval of its message, its edifying effect upon the public. Not only did the great philosopher perceive that poets and artists are habitual corrupters of youth and impious portrayers of their superiors, but they "persuade our youth that the Gods are authors of evil, and that heroes are no better than men." In other words, they tend to level societies based on principles of social hierarchy. Diamond compares the authentic artist to the Trickster of primitive cultures, a creature devoid of normal values, knowing neither good nor evil, yet constantly seeking the source of both.

> In his never ending search for himself, Trickster changes shape, and experiments with a thousand identities. He has enormous power, is enormously stupid, is "creator and destroyer, giver and negator." He is archetype of the comic spirit, the burlesque of the problem of identity, the ancestor of the clown, the fool of the ages.[23]

Plato would see to it that Trickster is tamed to "sing songs of the heroes." Hence in a more sophisticated culture Trickster is constrained to produce art that harmonizes with the existing power structure. In our case social myth implies that the divine right of money *is* power, and our "sacred places" — including our museums — are a celebration of that fact. For societies such as Plato's Republic the greatest dangers are always within, because their most extreme contradictions are invested within their social mythologies.

One might ask how the Guggenheim Museum induces the wealthy to contribute, carries off spectacular social events and openings, involves itself in intricate negotiations for purchases and sales of art, and then insists, as Thomas Messer has, that the Museum is "not competent" to comment on social ills? In reality any public or semi-public institution is an *a priori* symbol of power and authority. The museum's avowed duty is to choose and possess the superior artifacts of our culture. But what if these turn out to be floor sweeping compound, florescent lights, or typed filing cards? Beauty, at any rate, is no longer an issue. What is relevant is demolishing the fiction that appropriateness within a museum and the Trickster's function as artist are synonymous. Trickster is always on the side of the mob, although it may appear that he is playing a solo part. His natural targets are the values at the apex of Plato's Republic; similarly in primitive ritual dramas, "it is the thing which is regarded with the greatest reverence or respect which is ridiculed."[24] Trickster's psychic effectiveness lies in the sly obviousness of his inversions, while the psychic power of the ruling class exists in its ability to maintain the fiction that it alone is "competent." When Messer, speaking for the Museum, specifies that it is "not competent" to analyze social problems, what he is implying in effect is that the artist — as one of the ignorant multitude — has overstepped his bounds in assuming that *he is*.

In March and April of 1974, almost exactly three years after the Guggenheim affair, Haacke exhibited a set of brass-framed charts detailing the Solomon R. Guggenheim Museum's Board of Trustees and their corporate affiliations. What comes to light are the interlocking ties between two of the trustees and the Kennecott Copper Corporation. Haacke's panels reveal that the President of the Guggenheim Board of Trustees, Peter O. Lawson-Johnston, is a member of the Kennecott Board of Directors; inversely, the President and Chief Executive Officer of Kennecott, Frank R. Milliken, is a member of the Board of Trustees of the Guggenheim Museum. In his allusions to Kennecott's expropriated copper mines in Chile, Haacke quotes President Salvador Allende's address to the United Nations in 1972 as accusing the multinational companies of the International Telephone & Telegraph Corp. and the Kennecott Corp. of having "dug their claws into my country." Haacke also notes that the Military Junta of Chile, after the coup of Sept. 11th, 1973, committed itself to compensating Kennecott for its nationalized property, which was seized by Allende's Government in July of 1971 through the power of the Constitutional Reform Law, with the backing of all Chilian political parties.

For the museums Haacke's art represents something of a Hobson's choice; if they accept it, it constitutes to some degree, but not always, a form of self-indictment; if they reject it for specious reasons, usually the ensuing publicity is far more revealing than a

13 Daniel Buren incorporating *Manet-PROJEKT'74* facsimiles in his work at PROJEKT'74, Kunsthalle Köln, during opening July 5, 1974.

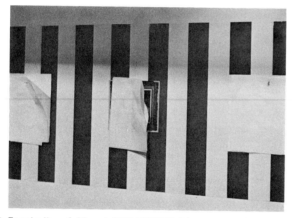

14 Facsimile of *Manet-PROJEKT'74* (then part of Daniel Buren's work) pasted over by order of Prof. Dr. Gerd von der Osten, Director of the Cologne Museums, July 6, 1974.

forthright statement could have been. There are occasions such as Haacke's exhibition at the Museum Haus Lange of the City of Krefeld, West Germany (1972) where the dynamics are somewhat different. The artist analyzed and displayed raw sewage pouring into the Rhine River from the Krefeld sewage plant. In this instance the museum's director, a civil servant, was entirely sympathetic with Haacke's ecological intentions, and thus a certain dialectical tension is missing from the piece. One reporter in a Krefeld newspaper noted that some of Haackes art transcends the art world and has civic implications. On telephoning the local official responsible for environmental protection and asking what response his agency would have to the problem, he was told, "My god, who goes there [to the museum] anyhow?" Museums may be able to afford

the piety of ecological ideals because these are issues that do not concern them directly.

Haacke's display of the provenance of Manet's *Bunch of Asparagus* (1880) for "PROJEKT '74" in Cologne is another instance of cultural hierarchies revealing themselves through clumsy attempts by officials to suppress imagined inflammatory information. In this case irony is piled upon irony. The Director of the Museum, in his frantic attempts to prevent the provenance from being shown, thus focussing attention on the well-known background of one of the Cologne Wallraf-Richartz-Museum's chief benefactors, Herman J. Abs, instigated a nation-wide controversy in the West German newspapers. The concluding irony is that, as Haacke and others suspect, the banker Herman J. Abs could not have cared less. The elegance of Haacke's best political works lies in their *indirection*, their ability to reveal without polemics or political slogans.

It should be added that in spite of the rejection, Haacke's provenance of the Manet was shown in "PROJEKT '74". Daniel Buren, the French artist, asked Haacke for a scaled down facsimile of the piece which Buren then proceeded to paste over the entire length of a wall of his vertical stripes in the Kunsthalle. Buren flanked this with an earlier statement of his concerning the role of museums in society, which was apropos to this situation, on a large poster which read, "*Kunst bleibt Politik*," a play on the theme of "PROJEKT '74", *Kunst bleibt Kunst*" ("Art remains art"). The collaged facsimiles remained during the exhibition's opening, but the following morning by order of the Director they were each pasted over with two sheets of typewriter paper. The cover-ups remained throughout the exhibition, although some were torn off by curious viewers. Buren added a declaration publicly explaining the situation and denouncing the actions of the museum.

Haacke's art continues its own unique dialectic of countering response with response. When recently asked to describe the present situation of a socially concerned artist, Haacke quoted Bertold Brecht's 1934 appraisal of the "Five Difficulties in Writing the Truth": "They are the need for "the courage to write the truth, although it is being suppressed; the intelligence to recognize it, although it is being covered up; the judgement to chose those in whose hands it becomes effective; the cunning to spread it among them".[25] Another remark of Brecht's comes to mind: "*Die Wahrheit muss auch schön sein*" ("The truth must also be beautiful.") In other words, the revelation of social fact must have its own elegance.

Notes

1. Egbert, Donald Drew, *Social Radicalism and the Arts: Western Europe,* New York: Alfred A. Knopf, 1970, pp. 364-378.
2. Quoted from a letter by Haacke to the writer, dated April 10, 1968.
3. Quoted from a letter by Haacke to the writer, dated April 28, 1968.
4. "Atelier populaire oui; Atelier bourgeois non" from *Posters from the Revolution, Paris, May 1968 (Mai 68: début d'une lutte prolongée),* (First published in 1969 by Dobson Books Ltd., London), Indianapolis, New York: The Bobbs-Merrill Co., Inc., 1971, pages not numbered.
5. Quoted from a letter by Haacke to the writer, dated April 10, 1968.
6. Glueck, Grace, "No Rush for Reservations," *Art Notes: The New York Times,* Sunday, July 5, 1969.
7. Quoted from a position paper written by artists, Fellows, and Director of the Center for Advanced Visual Studies at the Massachusetts Institute of Technology, Cambridge, Massachusetts, June 30, 1969.
8. Quoted from a letter by Dore Ashton to the writer, dated June 19, 1969.
9. Quoted from a letter by Haacke to the writer, dated April 22, 1969.
10. Haacke, Hans, "Provisional Remarks," essay published in German translation in *Hans Haacke: Werkmonographie,* Introduction Edward F. Fry, Dumont Schauberg, Cologne, 1972, p. 60.
11. Bertalanffy, Ludwig von, *General Systems Theory: Foundations, Development, Application,* New York: George Braziller, Inc., 1968.
12. *Ibid.,* p. 70.
13. Boguslaw, Robert, The New Utopian: *A Study of System Design and Social Change,* Englewood Cliffs, N.J.: Prentice Hall, Inc., 1965, p. 39.
14. Churchman, C. West, *The Systems Approach,* New York: Delacorte Press, 1968, pp. 28-36.
15. *Ibid.,* p. 196.
16. Marx, Karl, *Capital* (Translated by Samuel Moore and Edward Aveling), Chicago: Charles H. Kerr & Co., 1906, v. I, Book I, p. 81.
17. Catalogue for the exhibition *Art into Society: Society into Art, Seven German Artists.* Albrecht D., Joseph Beuys, KP Brehmer, Hans Haacke, Dieter Hacker, Gustav Metzger, Klaus Staeck, sponsored by the Institute of Contemporary Arts, London, October 30 - November 24, 1974, p. 63.
18. From a taped conversation between Haacke and the writer, May 4, 1975.
19. Messer, Thomas R., Director of The Solomon R. Guggenheim Museum, "Guest Editorial," *Arts Magazine,* New York, June 1971, pp. 4-5.
20. *Ibid.,* p. 5.
21. Diamond, Stanley, "Plato and the Definition of the Primitive" in *Primitive View of the World* (edited by Stanley Diamond), New York and London: Columbia University Press, 1960, p. 180.
22. Herzig, Doris, "Art show scrubbed as politically dirty," *Newsday,* Friday, April 9, 1971, p. 15A.
23. Diamond, "Plato and the . . . .", p. 182.
24. *Ibid.,* p. 190.
25. Catalogue for the exhibition *Art into Society: Society into Art . . .* p. 63.

Notes on Illustrations

1 *Condensation Cube*, 1963/65. 12″ × 12″ × 12″ (30×30×30cm), acrylic plastic, water, light, airdrafts, temperature in area of display.
First exhibited Galerie Schmela, Düsseldorf, May 1965. Edition of 10.

2 *Live Airborne System*, 1965/68. Photo of sea gulls attracted by bread that was thrown out on the ocean at Coney Island, New York, November 30, 1968.
Notes for project from 1965.

3 *Grass Grows*, 1967/69. View of installation during *Earth Art* exhibition at Andrew Dickson White Museum, Cornell University, Ithaca, N.Y., February 1969; director Thomas W. Leavitt, assisted by Willoughby Sharp. Soil was piled up and seeded.

4 *Circulation*, 1969. Vinyl hoses of three different diameters, Y-connectors, circulating pump with electric motor.
Installation view of group show *Earth, Air, Fire, Water: Elements of Art,* Museum of Fine Arts, Boston, 1971, guest-curator Virginia Gunther, director Perry Rathbone.
First exhibited one-man show at Howard Wise Gallery, New York, November 1969.

5 *Gallery-Goers' Birthplace and Residence Profile, Part 1*, 1969. The visitors of a one-man show at the Howard Wise Gallery, New York, November 1969, were requested to mark with pins their birthplace and their residence on large maps of New York, the area within 50 miles of New York City, the United States and the world.
Photograph: Robert E. Mates and Paul Katz, New York.
Owned by H.H.

6 *Gallery Goers' Residence Profile, Part 2,* 1970. View of installation, exhibition at Paul Maenz Gallery, Cologne, January 1971. 735 photographs, taken at all locations on Manhattan map marked as residences by visitors of Haacke exhibition at Howard Wise Gallery, New York, November 1969, are mounted with pins on the wall. Installation schematically follows north-south/left-right and east-west/ceiling-floor layout of Manhattan, with Fifth Avenue as an horizontal axis. Each vertical row of photographs represents a street. The street-blocks in question are listed on typewritten cards positioned in the horizontal axis.
Owned by H.H.

7 *On Sale at the Foundation Maeght.* Excerpt of manuscript for performance, during one of the *Nuits de la Fondation Maeght,* July 26, 1970, St. Paul de Vence, France. Part of exhibition *L'art vivant américain,* also with performances by Bob Israel and Robert Whitman; guest curator Dore Ashton.
A female voice read over the loudspeakers of the theatre, titles and prices of representative original prints on sale at the bookstore of the Fondation Maeght, a non-profit organization. All prints were from artists of the Galerie Maeght, Paris. Their aggregate value amounted to over $190,000. The reading of price quotations was interrupted regularly by a male voice which transmitted over the telephone, from the *Nice-Matin* newspaper office, incoming teletype messages from the wires of Agence France Press. During the reading Jean-Louis Prat, the director of the

Fondation, demanded an immediate stop to the performance. As he was not prepared to explain his reasons to the audience, the performance, with the collaboration of the sound-engineer, was completed as planned.

8 *10 Turtles Set Free*, June 20, 1970, woods near St. Paul de Vence, France.

9 *News,* 1969/70. View of installation at *Software* show, Jewish Museum, New York, September 1970; guest curator Jack Burnham, director Karl Katz. Exhibition sponsored by American Motors Corp. under the guidance of Ruder & Finn Fine Arts, Inc., a New York public relations company. 5 teletype machines hooked to the news wires of ANSA, Deutsche Presse Agentur, The New York Times, Reuters, and United Press International, produced printouts of transmitted messages throughout time of exhibition.
First exhibition with one teletype printer (news wire of Deutsche Presse Agentur) at *Prospect* 1969, Kunsthalle Düsseldorf; director Karl Ruhrberg.

9 *Shapolsky et al Manhattan Real Estate Holdings, a Real-Time Social System, as of May 1, 1971.* Excerpt. Work comprises map with properties marked, 142 photographs (8″ × 10″ / 20.3 × 25.4cm) of all building facades and empty lots, typewritten data sheets attached to each photograph giving address, block and lot number, lot size, and nature of building (building code), corporation or individual holding title, corporate address, corporations' officers, date of acquisition, prior owner, amount of mortgage, interest rate, mortgagee, assessed value. Also charts on the business relationships (frequent self-dealing with sales and mortgages) between individuals and some 70 corporations comprising the real estate group.
Properties are predominantly on the Lower East Side and in Harlem. They represent the largest real estate holdings in those areas.
Director Thomas Messer of the Solomon R. Guggenheim Museum rejected the work for exhibition in a scheduled one-man show, 1971. First exhibited in one-man show at Françoise Lambert Gallery, Milan, 1972. First U.S. exhibition in group show, *Making Megalopolis Matter,* October 1972, at New York Cultural Center; director Mario Amaya.
Edition of 2. One copy coll. Françoise Lambert, art dealer, Milan, other owned by H.H.

10 *Sol Goldman and Alex DiLorenzo Manhattan Real Estate Holdings, a Real-Time Social System, as of May 1, 1971.* Detail of Manhattan map with properties marked. Work comprises map, photographs of about 350 building facades or empty lots (contact prints), typewritten data giving address, block and lot number, lot size and nature of building (building code), corporation or individual holding title, date of acquisition, assessed value. Also a list of the 19 corporations operating the properties of the partnership of Sol Goldman and Alex DiLorenzo.
They represent the largest private real estate holdings in Manhattan. The market value of the properties was estimated by *Forbes* (June 1, 1971) at $666.7-million. New York law enforcement agencies suspect connection of partnership with organized crime.
Director Thomas Messer of the Solomon R. Guggenheim Museum rejected the work, 1971, for exhibition in

scheduled one-man show. First exhibited in group show *Prospect,* 1969, organized by Konrad Fischer, Jürgen Harten, Hans Strelow at Kunsthalle Düsseldorf; director Karl Ruhrberg. First U.S. exhibition in group show *Making Megalopolis Matter,* October 1972, at New York Cultural Center, director Mario Amaya.

Edition of 2. One copy coll. Sol LeWitt, artist, New York, other H.H.

11 *Krefeld Sewage Triptych,* 1972. Center Panel. Photo taken January 21, 1972 in Krefeld-Uerdingen, at Rhine kilometer mark 765.7, where City of Krefeld yearly discharges 42-million cubic meters of untreated sewage into the river.

Left panel lists data on volume, rate of pollution (official code), breakdown into industrial and household sewage, fees charged per volume. Right panel lists data on volume of deposable and dissolved matter, and breakdown by volume and name of major contributors of Krefeld sewage.

First exhibited summer 1972 in one-man show, Museum Haus Lange, Krefeld, Germany, a municipal museum under the directorship of Dr. Paul Wember.

Owned by H.H.

12 *Rhine-Water Purification Plant*, 1972. View of Installation in one-man show at Museum Haus Lange, Krefeld, summer 1972; director Dr. Paul Wember.

From large glass bottles, extremely polluted Rhine-water was pumped into an elevated acrylic basin. The injection of chemicals caused the pollutants to settle. The sedimentation process continued in a second acrylic container. From there the partially purified water flowed through a charcoal and a sandfilter and eventually dropped into a large basin with goldfish. A hose carried the overflow out to the garden, where it seeped into the ground and joined the groundwater level.

Development of the plant was assisted by Raimund Schröder of the Kaiser-Wilhelm-Museum, Krefeld, and Ernst Tiessen of the Stadtwerke Krefeld.

13 Daniel Buren incorporating *Manet-PROJEKT'74* facsimiles in his work at PROJEKT'74, Kunsthalle Köln, during opening July 5, 1974.

Photo: Barbara Reise

14 Facsimile of *Manet-PROJEKT'74* (then part of Daniel Buren's work) pasted over by order of Prof Dr. Gerd von der Osten, Director of the Cologne Museums, July 6, 1974.

Photo: Barbara Reise

Howard S. Becker and John Walton

Social Science and the Work of Hans Haacke

Hans Haacke's works resemble those of social scientists sufficiently to make comparison both provocative and illuminating: provocative because Haacke's work manages to make so much more of a stir than the social science research it superficially resembles; illuminating because the differences beneath the similarity arise from and tell us something of the organizational differences between the worlds of art and social science.

Even if Haacke imitated in every detail the methods of social scientists his work would still be different. Any work gets its meaning from the traditions and organized practice of the people among whom it is made and to whom it is presented. The same work makes a different statement, is a different act, when it appears in an art world rather than the world of social science. Haacke, speaking to artists, curators, collectors, gallery goers, critics and museum trustees, gets a different effect from the social scientist who speaks largely to other social scientists.

Despite these crucial differences, when Haacke investigates art as a social system, social scientists can interpret the results in the light of the traditions and organized practices of their scientific world. When we do that, we find ways of assessing Haacke's work that are unavailable within the art world proper. We likewise find that Haacke's "naive" social science uses interesting possibilities social scientists have not used, but might want to try.

In what follows, then, we view Haacke both as artist (i.e., as a participant in the art world whose activities he investigates) and a social scientist (i.e., as someone whose work can be viewed as an attempt to answer questions posed by social science theories and interests). This will do some violence to the conceptions readers hold of both art and social science, which is probably a good thing.

Methods of Studying Power

Haacke is mainly interested in the networks of relationships through which power is exercised in the art world and in the social, economic and political bases of that power. He has explored that interest in a variety of projects reproduced in this book: studies of elites and their interconnections, studies of the provenance of paintings, studies of the social characteristics and attitudes of patrons of museums and galleries, and even (one might say) experimental studies of the activities of museum directors. His earlier studies of physical and biological phenomena relied heavily on the idea of *system*, and he has brought that concern to his studies of social phenomena as well.

Social scientists have used many methods to bring empirical data to bear on their theories about the distribution and exercise of power. For more than twenty years books and papers have appeared which identified the topic as *The Power Elite* (Mills, 1956), *The Power Structure* (Rose, 1967), *Community Power Structure* (Hunter, 1953), and so on. This vast literature has never given a definitive answer to the question of how to study power. But it has had the consequence of introducing the idea of and the term "power structure" into common parlance. Without question, the term refers to something that makes intuitive sense to people with either a theoretical or practical interest in politics.

Speaking confidently of "power structures," social scientists promised what they never delivered: an explicit set of principles and procedures for the analysis of power. The failure to produce generally acceptable principles and procedures shows up in two ways. First, researchers, all claiming to study "power," have actually studied a great variety of things, ranging from personal influence in small face-to-face groups to corporate concentration, trends toward oligopoly, and the military-industrial complex. Second, researchers cannot agree on either methodological questions — should the unit of analysis be the individual or the institution — or ideological ones — is power distributed pluralistically or centered in elites?

Questions of theory, method and ideology are interrelated. Scientists trained in different disciplines use different methods, make different theoretical assumptions, and arrive at different conclusions and different ideological positions (Walton, 1966). If we consider the major approaches researchers have used, we can lay out the issues and assumptions involved, and place Haacke's work in relation to the social science tradition. We will set aside for the moment our awareness that Haacke is, after all, an artist producing works of

145

art, and see what we can learn if we consider him a social scientist producing research.

Where some of Haacke's procedures appear amateurish or inadequate in the light of some notion of an acceptable social science standard, we propose to be pragmatic in assessing his results. If the method used produces convincing results, then we will not require Haacke to use all the methods of verification, all the safeguards against bias or error, all the rigorous and systematic procedures social scientists have devised to guarantee to one another and the public the validity of their results. Social scientists in fact do this themselves, because of the lack of consensus on methods just alluded to. This means that Haacke's work cannot be held to account, as some might attempt to do, for failing to be conducted according to rigorous scientific standards. No such agreed on standards exist and, while there are certain well known precautions for avoiding bias, the practical constraints of the research situation (e.g., inaccessible or unavailable evidence) frequently require that the investigator make do with what data is obtainable — a practice recognized as justified as long as the researcher frankly reports the limitations imposed. Where the findings overwhelmingly point to a conclusion, a failure to use available safeguards against error makes little difference; the results may be so conclusive that even these potential errors would not change our interpretations, as some of the discussion below will make clear.

Social scientists studying power structure have used several distinctive procedures. Some use the individual as the unit of analysis, asking *who* is powerful or influential, *who* participates in the decision making process, what the social and occupational backgrounds of the influential are, what constituencies they represent. The *positional method,* for instance, begins with a set of offices or positions assumed to be important: members of Congress (Matthews, 1954), elected officials, judges, heads of large banks and corporations (Baron, 1968), or members of such decision making bodies as the President's Cabinet, the Council on Foreign Relations, and so on (Domhoff, 1970). The researcher uses available sources to report on the social backgrounds and interconnections of the people who occupy these positions (he may also interview them to get information not already available). Domhoff, for instance, concludes that U.S. politics is dominated by the "Higher Circles" of the upper class since a large proportion of holders of high positions are also listed in the Social Register or have other "blue blood" attributes.

Sociometric or reputational methods (Hunter, 1953; Miller, 1958) are similar though more elaborate aiming at the identification of who is "really" powerful whether those persons hold formal positions or operate "behind the scene." This procedure begins with a small panel of experts who hold a variety of positions in a community such that they may be presumed to be knowledgeable about local matters. This panel then is asked to identify the most important persons in town "when it comes to getting things done" or "promoting a major project." Tabulation of the nominations of this panel leads to a list of the highest vote-getters who are then designated as "influentials." Typically a second stage of this method involves interviewing the influentials to determine backgrounds, occupations, acquaintance with one another, and actual participation in local activities.

Organizational network methods take a similar approach but focus on the organization rather than the individual. Using this method, you identify key institutions, such as the largest banks and the largest non-financial institutions, and then determine the number of "interlocking directorates" linking them (the number of people holding directorships in two or more major institutions, e.g., Dye, et al., 1973). One can also use such economic data as how much of a given corporation is owned or controlled by a given bank or family grouping (Knowles, 1973; Zeitlin, 1974).

Haacke's Guggenheim piece uses a version of these methods, tracing family memberships and corporate directorships to show the dependence of the Guggenheim Museum on Guggenheim family financial interests and the implication of those interests in the exploitation of the mineral wealth of underdeveloped countries. In particular, Haacke uses this form of research to indicate the role of one of the Guggenheim companies, Kennecott Copper, in the economy of Allende's Chile. In doing this, Haacke uses none of the elaborate forms of analysis characteristic of power structure studies in social science. Since all the facts can obviously be checked in public records by anyone who wants to take the trouble, their authenticity need not be guaranteed by any rigorous method of data gathering. Since he draws no conclusion, letting "the facts speak for themselves," no one can complain that his methods of manipulating data do not warrant his conclusion.

Social scientists also make use of *decisional methods* or *event analysis* (Dahl, 1961). These methods criticize those just discussed for their reliance on mere reputations for power instead of on observations of the actual exercise of power. Decisional methods focus on key decisions and reconstruct their histories, seeking to discover who participated in making them. Analysts study several important decisions, to see whether the same people exercise power in all cases or whether the decision making elite consists of different people for each issue or area of politics. *Historical analyses* (Mills, 1956) do the same thing at the institutional level, trying to assess the shifting influence of major organizations and social sectors on large scale social policy. How, for example, do such major social changes as war, depression, expanding governmental bureaucracy or corporate concentration affect the distribution and exercise of social power? Mills argued, for instance, that power in America had increasingly centered on the military, the higher levels of the federal executive and the large corporations and documented his contention by tracing social backgrounds, common affiliations (e.g., prep schools, colleges and clubs), and individual careers that moved from the military to corporate vice-presidencies or from industry to related federal regulatory agencies.

Haacke has not used either of these methods in anything like their original form. One might argue, however, that the provenances of the Manet and Seurat paintings are a form of event analysis, which show the sequence of events that constitute the career of a particular art work and indicate the influential people who helped the work become historically important. The provenance, of course, relies almost entirely on publically available data (from *Who's Who,* reports of art auctions and the like) and does not actually provide information on who decided to do what in relation to the work or the influences on those decisions. In that sense it does not go as far as event analyses usually do to remedy the complaint that while powerholders have been identified we do not see how they exercise their power, under what conditions and to what ends. We learn that Feigen, Berggruen and Artemis S.A. collaborated in an elaborate sequence of events leading to the most recent disposal of the Seurat painting, but not who decided that it should be done that way or for what reason (though we have plenty of material of which to base a guess).

In this case, Haacke has followed one sort of analytic tradition in relying solely on publically verifiable data which do not require interpretation to be used. Another tradition would have required him to interview Feigen, Berggruen and others on the board of Artemis S.A., perhaps to gain access to their private meetings, and so to have become privy to the most minute aspects of this sale, of the interactions between participants, and to their private and collective thinking about what they were doing, had done and were about to do. Practically, such a method might not be possible, for it depends on the participants granting the investigator access to ordinarily private affairs, and such permission would presumably not have been granted in this and similar cases. Indirect methods of gathering data, which require much more interpretive inference, are often necessary, but are naturally less useful.

One might also argue that Haacke used a form of experimental event analysis in the occurrences that followed the cancellation of his show at the Guggenheim Museum. He may not have intended, by offering to exhibit works depicting the social system of certain real estate holdings in Manhattan, to provoke the museum director into cancelling his scheduled show. But that was the result. The cancellation led to the firing of the museum curator, to the boycott of the museum by many artists and, it has been argued, to a living demonstration of "the character of the cultural establishment within which artists have been forced to function" (Fry, 1972). This vivid demonstration may not reflect direct pressure from the museum's trustees; Haacke himself thinks not, believing that subordinates often pursue their principals' interests more zealously than the principals themselves would. Nevertheless, it does demonstrate the exercise of power in the contemporary art world and thus provides important data about the process as well as the location of power.

In addition, Haacke has considered two aspects of power ordinarily included in social science theorizing about power, but seldom included in the research agendas that flow from the theories. Theories of power frequently allude to the relationship between the powerful and the powerless, suggesting that we understand power only when we understand the basis on which its subjects allow it to be exercised (Weber, 1957). Theorists draw distinctions between power which is accepted as legitimate — authority — and coercive power, whose subjects do not recognize its legitimacy. But research seldom investigates the attitudes of the subjects of power. It would stretch matters somewhat to regard the polls Haacke conducted as investigations of the attitudes of powerless subjects of the rulers of the art world. But the polls do indicate that gallery goers overwhelmingly favor left-liberal causes, positions and candidates, that they do not provide the financial underpinings of the art world by purchasing art works, that they mistrust the wealthier people who do provide that support, and that they are in large measure people with some sort of professional interest in art.

These conclusions give us useful material on the ideological arrangements of the art world, on the relations of beliefs and social position, and on the degree to which those without power live in a world made by people who believe very differently from them. The other end of the ideological structure is documented in the plates displaying the thinking of Nixon, Rockefeller, and others on the relations between art and business.

In what sense can these polls and quotations from speeches and corporate documents provide sufficient data of a quality to allow us to draw valid conclusions about the contemporary art world? It is clear enough in the case of the polls that Haacke has not followed standard procedures of questionnaire construction, sampling or analysis. The questions, not by their wording but by the kinds of materials they probe, suggest strongly to the respondent the political position from which they emanate, and this conceivably might prompt some to answer in ways they think pleasing to the questionnaire's author, or vice versa. The analysis never proceeds beyond simple cross tabulations or the answers to two questions. The samples consist of visitors to a gallery, some portion of whom answered the questionnaire; it is not known whether the non-respondents differ in any important way, such as might influence their answers, from those who did fill out the instruments.

These all constitute flaws in Haacke's procedures but, in our judgment, not of sufficient magnitude to cast serious doubt on the conclusions we have already mentioned as indicated by the data. He has, first of all, followed scientific practice scrupulously in indicating all the circumstances of the polling, such that a skeptical reader knows all the precautions that need to be taken in interpreting the data and could even replicate the research if that was thought necessary. Though social science textbooks contain a multitude of rules about how research should be done, these rules are often impractical and cannot be followed exactly in the real world situations in which research is done. In that case, working scientists do essentially what Haacke has done: do the best they can and inform the reader so that the findings may be discounted accordingly.

Secondly, Haacke's findings are very clearcut. Many of the more elaborate procedures of survey design, sampling and analysis are designed to allow the researcher to "tease out" (a suggestive phrase) findings from data which show no clearcut pattern. When the poll shows that museum goers disapprove Rockefeller's policies by a ratio of two to one, it seems unlikely (on the basis of everything we know about museums and museumgoers, which is the basis on which working scientists make these judgments) that sampling errors or the wording of the questions account for these results. It is not plausible that the full population of museumgoers, had they answered, or that the population that did answer, had they been confronted with a question that sounded more pro-Rockefeller, would have produced data that showed that they were evenly divided for and against or that the majority actually favored Rockefeller's position.

The quotations from business and political leaders are made to stand for the ideology with respect to art of that segment of the American power elite. Haacke has here made use of a powerful device often used by social scientists, though seldom formally described as a "method." The device consists of demonstrating incontrovertibly that some event or utterance occured even once, and then arguing that the conditions under which this happened are such that it must be a common occurrence, built into the fabric of the organization or society in which it happened. The demonstration is especially effective if it can be shown or argued that

when the event occurred no one thought it very remarkable or out of line, but rather that it was accepted as an everyday and ordinary event; that can be accomplished when the reader understands that, had the event been out of the ordinary, some outcry would have followed. In the case of the plaques, we can see that these are the kind of statements political and business leaders make all the time. We know, further, that we have heard no one complain about these remarks, which enhances our willingness to accept them as straightforward evidence of the ideology about art current in the business and political communities.

Beyond the parallels between Haacke's methods and those of social scientists it is important to stress that each has something to learn from the other. Haacke may have made a contribution to social science method by adapting the art historical technique of the provenance to the study of power. We can describe the technique more generally as one of following the history of ownership of a socially valued object (its "career"), thus tracing the outlines of some portion of an elite network; this is analogous to the way following an individual's career traces the outlines of a professional organization (cf. Hughes, 1971, pp. 132-150). This becomes more interesting when the objects traced begin with little value and gradually accumulate more, thus penetrating successively higher elite circles. Perhaps this method has not occurred to social scientists because there are few social objects whose value continually increases as that of some art works does. On the other hand, a great many objects continually lose value (for instance most cars) and these might make possible the use of a reverse form of the method.

In summary, Haacke has made reasonable use of variants of social science methods. His results are credible and acceptable by social science standards. Like many good social scientists, he has viewed the phenomena he studies as connected in a *system*. This had led him to the use of the multiple methods we have just reviewed and assessed, by means of which he can gather data on a variety of participants and events in the art world and give them, viewed as a system, more meaning than any one set of findings would have alone. The findings of each individual inquiry both rest on and reinforce the findings of all the other works, so that the analysis of the system, considered as a whole, is more credible than any one set of findings might be. (The logic of this kind of holistic analysis is explicated in Diesing, 1971.)

Haacke's Theory of the Art World

Haacke has scrupulously refrained from enunciating an explicit theory of the social, political and economic organization of the contemporary art world. The data he has accumulated and presented nevertheless clearly embody such a theory. One practice of organized social science which may prove useful to his enterprise is the habit of summarizing and collating results in a general theoretical form. One puts the available material together and extrapolates from it, describing an entire system or even an entire class of theoretically defined phenomena as though it were what the partial data accumulated indicate it might be. The procedure allows you to see where your data are leading, where the gaps that require filling are, and makes it possible to identify data which show that the theory is wrong and thus allow it to be revised on an empirical basis.

Haacke has not made his theory explicit, so we will attempt a brief summary. The theory describes both the organization of the contemporary art world and the processes by which it is maintained. The bottom layer of the art world consists of a relatively large (compared to the numbers of participants at other levels) aggregate of gallery and museum goers, the "public" for contemporary art. These people are typically young, upper-middle class, politically interested and left-liberal in their politics, artists, art students or otherwise professionally involved in the arts. They believe that the major institutions of the art world (especially museums) are run by people of a different political stance — that museum trustees, for instance, were Nixon supporters while gallery goers supported McGovern — and that those institutions, accordingly, are not responsive to their desires and tastes — that gallery goers like or tolerate politically engaged art, but that museums will not exhibit it. The members of this stratum do not provide much financial support for contemporary art; despite their class position, they are young enough that they have not yet realized their income potential. But they believe that the preferences of the wealthier people who back the art world, people whose politics they understand to be well to the right of their own, influence the kind of work artists produce. The public for contemporary art, then, believes that the work it is most interested in is ultimately controlled by people who have a view of the art enterprise contradictory to their own.

The evidence of the plaques containing quotations from business and political leaders, especially the Rockefeller brothers, shows that the public's suspicions are not wrong. These leaders, who furnish the bulk of the money supporting contemporary art institutions, do indeed view art differently: Nelson Rockefeller thinks it has no intellectual (hence, no political) meaning; David Rockefeller describes art as a good investment for corporate business; Frank Stanton thinks art is essential to business. The Guggenheim study shows further that the members of this top stratum of the contemporary art world — the trustees of one of the most avant-garde museums — get the income they use to support art from exploitative and imperialist businesses of the kind members of that world's public abhor, in this case Kennecott Copper, whose involvement in the fate of Allende's Chile the Guggenheim panels document.

The cancellation of Haacke's Guggenheim show (which we will continue to interpret as one of his pieces of research) demonstrated, as did the events surrounding the cancellation of the exhibition of the Manet provenance in Cologne, the role of the functionaries of contemporary art institutions. They act to protect what they take to be the interests of their employers; it is possible, and even likely, that they over-react to the provocations offered by works such as Haacke's and that their trustees would not mind these exhibitions so much. (That supposition is something Haacke might check out in further works.) These events lay bare the process by which the financial control of art institutions actually affects the work of artists by controlling what is exhibited. Artists are presumably less likely to make works that are not acceptable to the major outlets in which they might be exhibited. Since the Haacke pieces that provoked these cancellations had political connotations, we can see the process by which politically meaningful work is institutionally discouraged. These events thus provide evidence that the public's belief that the work it finds interesting is discouraged by those who control contemporary art is correct.

The two provenances give information on another aspect of the contemporary art system, its financial arrangements. They suggest a number of conclusions. The two paintings appreciated enormously since they were created, and mostly in the past several years (the Seurat, purchased in 1936 for $40,000. sold for over a million dollars at an auction in 1970). The big jump in value came when the paintings ceased to be circulated among family members or a small group of upper-class acquaintances and moved into the open market. In these two cases, at least, while huge profits were made, the artists (long since dead) got no share of them. In both cases, the data suggest more elaborate financial arrangements than are explicitly described, but leave no doubt that investment for speculative gain is a major element. That, of course, is no news with respect to the market in contemporary art.

The irony involved in the case of the Manet merits remarking on. Here a man who was active in the financial affairs of Nazi Germany ends up arranging for the donation to a German museum of a painting held for many years by a German Jewish painter and finally brought to the U.S. by a prominent anti-Nazi refugee. It is not clear what the general theoretical import of this is.

Taken together, all of Haacke's materials seem to imply a theory that describes the contemporary art world as one organized around an endemic conflict between the interests of those who produce the art and the broader public which supports them ideologically, on the one hand, and the interests of the much smaller group of wealthy people and politicians who provide the big money supporting the system. Working through such intermediate institutional functionaries as museum directors, those who control the system act in various ways to control the output of artists and particularly to diminish and mute the political content of their work.

We think this is a fair summary of the theory implicit in Haacke's work. Much of the theory is at best *suggested* by the works Haacke has so far produced rather being demonstrated in any more compelling way. They do, however, touch on such key aspects of the contemporary art system, and such key persons in it, that the theory has a presumptive claim to acceptance. A social scientist might proceed by waiting to see what counter-assertions were made disputing the validity of his theoretical claims, then organizing future work so as to test the validity of those counter-assertions. We are not aware that anyone has actually disputed Haacke's findings. It would presumably be difficult to challenge the facts, since most of them are publically available and easily checked. People might dispute the implicit theory in Haacke's work. But, being implicit, it is hardly available for dispute. We are not sure to what degree Haacke is willing to assume responsibility for the theory we have read out of (or into) his work, or for some other theory that he finds more acceptable. Insofar as he disclaims responsibility for the interpretation (as he has in Siegel, 1971: "I leave it up to you as far as how you evaluate the situation. You continue the work by drawing your own conclusions from the information presented."), he makes it difficult to find the questions of validity which might orient future work.

But, of course, Haacke is not a social scientist; we have only been pretending that he is. He is an artist, and we now turn to a consideration of the *differences* between Haacke's work and that of social scientists, of the differences that are due to and illuminate the difference between the organized world of art in which Haacke operates and the organized world of social science in which studies of power are undertaken and presented. In short, we consider the two kinds of work as gestures that derive their meaning from the social worlds in which they occur.

Gestures in a Social World

Haacke, operating in an art world with methods and results in many ways similar to those of social scientists, gets very different and much more substantial reactions to his work than social scientists get, in their world, to their work. His work provokes reactions from relevant parties such that the reactions themselves provide further information about the original subject of the work, the exercise of power in the art world. In addition, the results of his work, having a kind of unarguably "valid" character, in fact are accepted by all the relevant parties as correct, which adds further to their provocative character.

Haacke's work has the appearance of unquestioned validity because the customary response of the art world to works of art no longer includes the possibility of questioning the veridicality of the statement the work makes. While appreciators of visual art could once include among the criteria by which they judged a work its faithfulness to the person or scene it purported to portray, the question of faithfulness is no longer of interest to anyone. We understand that a portrait, for instance, need not look anything like the person it portrays to be successful; it is enough that the image be formally interesting or emotionally compelling. (Photography has now acquired some of the burden of faithfulness to reality that painting and sculpture once carried; see Ivins, 1953, and Gombrich, 1960.) To say of a work of art, in any but the most extended metaphorical sense, that it is *not true,* is to make a meaningless remark.

Since the truth of an art work is not an issue, it follows that whatever else artists and critics discuss and argue about, the question of truth is not examined. Most contemporary works make little or no claim to truth; those that do tend to make the claim as Haacke's works do, by displaying facts that are regarded as self-evident and not requiring proof. Because the truth is self-evident, the meaning likewise is self-evident, and the steps by which one proceeds from fact to meaning need not be demonstrated or questioned. This is a rather tedious justification of Haacke's practice of drawing no explicit conclusions from his work, leaving that interpretive work as an exercise for the viewer. Confronted with the Guggenheim panels or the provenances, for instance, the viewer must search out the connections, keeping in mind in dealing with the data on the Elgerbar Corporation that Mrs. Obre was born a Guggenheim and that Wettach and Lawson-Johnston are her sons by other marriages, while Stewart is her brother-in-law, and drawing the conclusions that information seems to warrant. But the premises and logical procedures by which those conclusions are reached seem, to all concerned, to be obvious and beyond question.

The reason we have been so tedious and longwinded on this point is because customary practice in the world of social science is very different, and because the difference has important consequences for the impact of the work. Haacke's work has great impact in its world because his conclusions are unquestioned. But no social science conclusion, particularly when the subject is of contemporary political interest, goes unquestioned and it is only extremely rarely that the questioning is ever resolved into some kind of consensus of the scientific community. Social scientists question sources of data, procedures of analysis, interpretations, premises, assumptions — whatever can conceivably be questioned. They regard all conclusions as provisional. As a result, anyone who finds a particular conclusion or interpretation annoying or threatening can easily find a social scientist of as good reputation as the author of the distasteful conclusion to dispute it, to produce a counter-conclusion, to produce data which threaten the validity of the unwanted result. If Mills (1956) and Hunter (1953) find that American society is dominated by a power elite, Rose (1967) and Dahl (1961) can be adduced in support of the conclusion that no power elite exists because America is in fact a pluralist society.

In short, Haacke's work provokes strong reactions because it appears, in some large part because of the conventional practices of the art world, as incontrovertible and patently true; no one questions it. It provokes those reactions for a second reason, which also requires a lengthy explanation.

Haacke presents his results in a way that openly flaunts the power of those whose power he exposes. The works he produces expose what the people implicated in them would presumably prefer not be exposed (if *exposed* is too strong a word, substitute *remind*). If, preferring that these things not be publicized, those involved cannot or do not stop the publicity, then they perhaps do not have the power they and others imagine they have. If, however, they do prevent the publicity, they can do so only by causing an even larger commotion in which not only the original materials are exposed, but also the attempt to suppress those materials. At its best, Haacke's work succeeds in presenting the powers-that-be of the contemporary art world with this Hobson's choice. In either case, what they do produces still further useful information about power in the art world.

We can remark on two aspects of this strategy and the reactions it provokes. First, what Haacke does can be conceived not as an exercise in power but rather as an exercise in bad taste. The powerful frequently view challenges to their power as lapses of etiquette (cf. Becker, 1970, pp. 8-11). Haacke provides an example (in Siegel, 1971, pp. 20-21):

Emily Genauer gave us a little glimpse of the larger base of the [MOMA poll of attitudes toward Rockefeller's political position] in her review of the show. She wrote: "One may wonder at the humor (propriety, obviously, is too archaic a concept even to consider) of such poll-taking in a museum founded by the governor's mother, headed now by his brother, and served by himself and other members of his family in important financial and ad-

ministrative capacities since its founding 40 years ago." With this little paragraph she provided some of the background for the work that was not intelligible for the politically less-informed visitors of the museum. She also articulated feelings that are shared by the top people at numerous museums. It goes like this: We are the guardians of culture. We honor artists by inviting them to show in *our* museum, we want them to behave like guests, proper, polite and grateful. After all, we have put up the dough for this place.

This works both ways. Defining a challenge to power as a lapse in taste is a way of denying its political import. Conversely, such a definition makes it possible to make a political statement out of an act of bad taste.

Second, this political challenge or failure to obey etiquette is possible because Haacke works in the same social space as those his work describes. His work thus differs profoundly from social science studies of the powerful, which typically occur as events in a world of social science quite separate from the world of the powerful people and organizations it describes. Haacke's work is displayed in, discussed in, is an event in an art world which includes among its integral elements (cf. Levine, 1972) the dealers, directors, trustees and collectors who appear in that very work. The subjects of power structure studies can ignore the books written about them because those books never impinge on or occur as events in the worlds they more in. They might think it in bad taste to find their corporate directorships discussed in detail, but they need not listen to such discussions or have their noses rubbed in their inability to prevent the discusssions from taking place. Academic research appears in esoteric professional journals, or in papers read at meetings attended by disciplinary colleagues. An occasional finding achieves a momentary publicity in the daily press, but not more than that. Academic social science is sufficiently segregated from the worlds it describes, by virtue of its conventional practice with respect to the publication and dissemination of results, that scientists do not have the means to offer such provocations as Haacke does. Since they can so seldom do that, they equally seldom provoke the responses which provide even further information.

It is a sign of how segregated academic social science is from the worlds it describes that it is even difficult to imagine how it could achieve the same results. One way would be for social scientists to do research on their own world, on the world of universities, and publicize the results in the internal communications of that world. Probably the nearest approach to that occured when people discovered and made public such matters as the character of contract research being done for the government by universities, the kinds of investments universities made with their funds, and the secret involvement of both universities and individual researchers with such government agencies as the Department of Defense and the CIA (eg., Horowitz, 1969; Ransom 1970). But those discoveries have not been followed up in succeeding and more systematic accounts of the nature of the university world; in that respect Veblen's *The Higher Learning in America,* written in 1918, is still not surpassed. This is not to deny the existence of a sizable literature in such areas as the sociology of science and university organization; nevertheless, we think it fair to say that hardly any of this literature confronts the members of these worlds with the facts of power in them as Haacke's work confronts the art community. The closest parallel we know of was a study of Columbia University, its trustees, real estate interests, and federal research grants, all of which indicated intimate linkages with the people and institutions Mills called the power elite (NACLA, 1968). But, again, we do not know of any virulent reaction to this research.

In any event, it is studies of community and national power to which this point is most relevant. We have imagined the following as a way of seeing what social scientists would have to do to achieve an effect equivalent to Haacke's. William Domhoff (1974) has written a book on the informal associations of the rich and powerful, centered about the members of an exclusive West Coast summer camp called Bohemian Grove. Supposing Domhoff were to present his tabulations on large posters, pasted on the walls of San Francisco's Pacific Union Club, another organization to which many of the same people belong. *That* would approximate what Haacke's works do to the art world, and presumably would produce consequences for Domhoff and his work equivalent to the cancellations and other phenomena which have accompanied Haacke's exhibitions.

We do not argue that academic social scientists should necessarily attempt to produce the same kinds of effects Haacke has. To discuss the advantages and disadvantages of such procedures for the development of science would take another essay as long as this one, and one more relevant to another kind of audience. Suffice it to say that the intimate involvement of the rich and powerful in the day-to-day workings of the contemporary art world have provided Haacke with a resource not available to the academic social scientist, whose work is so segregated from the centers of social power. He has used that resource to produce art works with a substantial social science content and interest.

References

Baron, Harold M., "Black Powerlessness in Chicago," *Trans-action*, 6 (November 1968), pp. 27-33.

Becker, Howard S., "The Struggle for Power on the Campus," in Howard S. Becker (ed.) *Campus Power Struggle* (Transaction, Inc.: 1970).

Dahl, Robert, *Who Governs?* (New Haven: Yale University Press, 1961).

Diesing, Paul, *Patterns of Discovery in the Social Sciences*, (Chicago: Aldine-Atherton, 1971).

Domhoff, G. William, *The Higher Circles: The Governing Class in America*, (New York: Vintage Books, 1970).

Domhoff, G. William, *The Bohemian Grove and Other Retreats: A Study in Ruling Class Cohesiveness*, (New York: Harper Row, 1974).

Dye, Thomas R., Eugene R. De Clercq, and John W. Pickering, "Concentration, Specialization, and Interlocking Among Institutional Elites," *Social Science Quarterly* 54 (June, 1973), pp. 8-28.

Fry, Edward, "The Post-Liberal Artist," *Art and Artists* (February, 1972), pp. 33-34.

Gombrich, E.H., *Art and Illusion: A Study in the Psychology of Pictorial Representation* (Princeton: Princeton University Press, 1960).

Horowitz, David, "Sinews of Empire," *Ramparts*, 8 (October, 1969), pp. 32-42.

Hughes, Everett C., *The Sociological Eye* (Chicago: Aldine-Atherton, 1971).

Hunter, Floyd, *Community Power Structure: A Study of Division Makers* (Chapel Hill: University of North Carolina Press, 1953).

Ivins, William Jr., *Prints and Visual Communication* (Cambridge: MIT Press, 1953).

Knowles, John C., "The Rockefeller Financial Group" in Ralph L. Andreano (ed.), *Super-concentration/Supercorporation: A Collage of Opinion on the Concentration of Economic Power* (Andover, Mass: Warner Modular Publications, 1973).

Levine, Edward M., "Chicago's Art World," *Urban Life and Culture*, 1 (1972), 292-322.

Matthews, Donald R., *Social Background of the Political Decision Makers* (Garden City, N.Y.: Doubleday, 1954).

Miller, Delbert C., "Decision Making Cliques in Community Power Structures: A Comparative Study of an American and an English City," *American Journal of Sociology*, 54 (November, 1958), pp. 299-309.

Mills, C. Wright, *The Power Elite* (New York: Oxford University Press, 1956).

NACLA (North American Congress on Latin America), "Who Rules Columbia?" (New York: NACLA, 1968).

Ransom, David, "The Berkeley Mafia and the Indonesian Massacre," *Ramparts*, 9 (October, 1970), pp. 27-29 and 40-49.

Rose, Arnold, *The Power Structure: Political Processes in American Society* (New York: Oxford University Press, 1967).

Siegel, Jeanne, "Interview with Hans Haacke," *Arts Magazine* (May, 1971), pp. 18-21.

Walton, John, "Discipline, Method, and Community Power: A Note on the Sociology of Knowledge," *American Sociological Review*, 31 (October, 1966), pp. 684-689.

Weber, Max, *The Theory of Social and Economic Organization*, Talcott Parsons, (ed.), (Glencoe: Free Press, 1957).

Zeitlin, Maurice, "Corporate Ownership and Control: The Large Corporation and the Capitalist Class," *American Journal of Sociology*, 79 (March, 1974) pp. 1073-1119.

On the Authors

Hans Haacke, born 1936 in Cologne, Germany. Equivalent of M.F.A. from Staatliche Werkakademie (State Art Academy), Kassel, 1960. With scholarship of DAAD (German Academic Exchange Service) work at Atelier 17, with S.W. Hayter in Paris, 1960. Fulbright Fellow, 1961, at Tyler School of Art, Temple University, Philadelphia, P.A. Since 1962, with 2 years interruption in Cologne, continuous residence in New York. 1973 Fellowship of John Simon Guggenheim Foundation. Teaching at Cooper Union, New York, since 1967, presently Associate Professor.

Jack W. Burnham, born New York City, 1931. Education: Boston Museum School of Fine Arts, Wentworth Institute, Boston, and M.F.A. from Yale University in 1961. Books: *Beyond Modern Sculpture,* 1968; *The Structure of Art,* 1971; *Great Western Salt Works,* 1974. Presently Associate Editor of *Arts* Magazine. Professor of Art at Northwestern University, Evanston, Illinois, and presently Dana Professor of Fine Arts at Colgate University, Hamilton, N.Y.

Howard S. Becker was born in Chicago in 1928 and received the Ph.D. in sociology from the University of Chicago in 1951. He has done research on drugs, medical students, college students and art. He teaches and practices photography and is a cardcarrying member of the American Federation of Musicians, Local 10-208. Since 1965, he has been Professor of Sociology at Northwestern University.

John Walton is Professor of Sociology and Urban Affairs at Northwestern University. He was born in Los Angeles in 1937 and received the Ph.D. in sociology from the University of California, Santa Barbara, in 1966. His research interests have been in political power, and third world development.